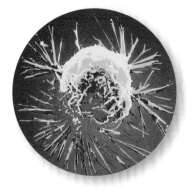

The Truth About Cancer
Understanding and Fighting
a Deadly Disease

ISSUES IN FOCUS TODAY

Kristi Lew

E **Enslow Publishers, Inc.**
40 Industrial Road
Box 398
Berkeley Heights, NJ 07922
USA

http://www.enslow.com

This book is dedicated to Mary Lumapas and her family, Gaythee, Fabian, and Rio. Your love, humor, and energy shine through. You guys are truly an inspiration.

Library of Congress Cataloging-in-Publication Data

Lew, Kristi.
 The truth about cancer : understanding and fighting a deadly disease / Kristi Lew.
  p. cm. — (Issues in focus today)
 Summary: "Examines the deadly disease cancer, including a history of the disease, diagnosis and treatment, coping with cancer, and the fight against it around the world"—Provided by publisher.
 Includes bibliographical references and index.
 ISBN-13: 978-0-7660-3068-8
 ISBN-10: 0-7660-3068-7
 1. Cancer—Juvenile literature. I. Title.
 RC264.L48 2009
 616.99′4—dc22
                                2008032026

Printed in the United States of America

10 9 8 7 6 5 4 3 2 1

To Our Readers: We have done our best to make sure all Internet addresses in this book were active and appropriate when we went to press. However, the author and the publisher have no control over and assume no liability for the material available on those Internet sites or on other Web sites they may link to. Any comments or suggestions can be sent by e-mail to comments@enslow.com or to the address on the back cover.

♻ Enslow Publishers, Inc. is committed to printing our books on recycled paper. The paper in every book contains between 10% to 30% post-consumer waste (PCW). The cover board on the outside of each book contains 100% PCW. Our goal is to do our part to help young people and the environment too!

Illustration Credits: Simon Lewandowski, p. 28; courtesy of the Lumapas family, pp. 3, 5, 7, 72, 93; Mike Mitchell/Dr. Bruce Chassey Laboratory, National Institute of Dental Research, pp. 84, 95; National Cancer Institute, pp. 1, 3, 9, 13, 27, 30, 33, 41, 47, 49, 55, 59, 65, 68, 75, 80, 87, 91; Photos.com, pp. 3, 21, 24; Rubberball Productions, pp. 3, 51, 61, 89; Shutterstock, pp. 3, 37, 44, 78; Wikimedia Commons, pp. 3, 18.

Cover Illustrations: National Cancer Institute (breast cancer cell); Banana Stock (small inset photo).

C o n t e n t s

Introduction

"Mary hated to be tickled," her mother, Gaythee Lumapas, remembers. "I just thought she was extra sensitive and did not like it."[1] But in fact it was painful for Mary when people tried to tickle her and put pressure on her abdomen. When Mary noticed blood in her urine, her mother knew something was wrong and that Mary needed to go to the doctor.

Mary was diagnosed with Wilms' tumor, a cancer of the kidney. She was just five years old. She had surgery and ten days of radiation treatment. This put her cancer into remission, which means that it disappeared. But when Mary was nine, she had a relapse. Her cancer had returned. This time, not only did she have to have surgery and radiation treatment, but she also had thirty-two rounds of chemotherapy (medication to kill cancer cells). Three years later, Mary now age twelve, is in remission again.

Wilms' tumor is named for Carl Max Wilhelm Wilms, the doctor who first recognized that the cancer developed in immature kidney cells. The kidneys are two bean-shaped organs, about the size of a fist, on either side of the backbone. They filter waste and extra water out of the bloodstream and convert it into urine. Wilms' tumor is a cancer that mostly affects children. It is usually found by the time a child is three years old. It rarely reoccurs after the age of eight.

Mary had trouble keeping fluids down during her chemotherapy. But it was very important for her to stay hydrated. She craved an ICEE, the slushy drink sold at convenience stores, but the hospital was far from her home. "I was not familiar with the town and I had no idea where to look for an ICEE," Mary's mother said.[2] But Mary is not easily discouraged, so she decided to start a petition drive to get All Children's Hospital in St. Petersburg, Florida, where she was being treated, to install an ICEE machine. And it worked! Today, children being treated at All Children's Hospital and their families still enjoy the tasty treats.

Getting an ICEE machine installed is not the only thing Mary did to help the children being treated at All Children's Hospital. Every year, the hospital holds a telethon to raise money. Mary decided she wanted to do some fund-raising, too. For her twelfth birthday, Mary held a huge garage sale instead of a birthday party. She sent out e-mails and letters asking for donations of money or merchandise for the garage sale. She also put out containers to collect change at gas stations, grocery stores, and drugstores in her community. She raised $12,385 for All Children's Hospital.

If you or a loved one has been diagnosed with cancer, Mary

Mary Lumapas and her family present a check representing the money she raised for All Children's Hospital in St. Petersburg, Florida.

suggests that you learn all you can about the illness. "Don't be afraid to talk to your doctors and to ask them questions," she says.[3] Gaythee has always been very honest with Mary about her treatments. So Mary knew that her hair would probably fall out while she was receiving chemotherapy, and she was not frightened when it happened. She also knew that it would grow back after the treatments stopped. Many people feel more in control when they know what is going to happen. "Knowledge is power," Mary says.[4]

Mary was diagnosed with Wilms' tumor for the second time when she was nine years old and in the fourth grade. When her treatments began, she became very ill, and it was hard for her to go to school. During this difficult time, Mary's brother, Rio, brought home all of her school assignments and notes from her teacher. "Rio was a huge help," Gaythee and Mary agree.[5] The following year, the school installed a camera in Mary's fifth-grade classroom so she could feel like she was a part of the class. Her teacher came to Mary's home a couple of times, too. But eventually it was just too hard for her to keep up with what was going on in the classroom while she was at home. So for the sixth grade, Mary went to a virtual school. Florida's Virtual School let Mary take classes online, at her own pace. She could structure her school time around treatments and she would not fall behind. For seventh grade, Mary will be going back to a regular public school. She is looking forward to it.

Breast cancer cell

What Is Cancer?

Cancer is often talked about as if it is only one disease. But it is really a group of more than two hundred related diseases.[1] Other than the fact that they all form in the same way, cancers can vary quite a lot. Some types of cancer are easier to treat, while others are more life-threatening. Some types grow aggressively; others almost never spread. All cancers have one thing in common—they started as one cell that grew and did not stop.

Cells Gone Wild

Every cell in your body is designed to do a particular job. With the exception of brain and nerve cells, all of your cells are constantly dividing. Eventually, they die and are replaced with more cells of their kind. The number of times a cell divides before it dies is determined by the chemical makeup of the cell. Scientists are not sure what causes some cells to die faster than others.[2] But if something disrupts the program that tells the cell whether to divide or die, the cell may keep dividing forever. And, sometimes, cells divide very quickly. A cell growing out of control is what causes cancer.

Cells divide for all sorts of reasons. They divide as an embryo grows into a baby and as a baby grows into an adult. They also divide in order to repair injuries, such as a scraped knee. Normal cells divide only when they receive a chemical signal to do so. Some cells, like blood and skin cells, divide throughout a person's life. Other cells, such as nerve and brain cells, stop dividing once the nervous system is fully formed.

Chemicals called growth factors tell cells whether to divide or not. These chemicals are sometimes produced when a cell comes into physical contact with another cell. The growth factors tell the cells that they need to stop growing because they are touching and have no more room to grow. Growth factors can also circulate in the bloodstream. For example, if a person is injured and loses blood, the body needs to produce more blood. So a growth factor produced by the kidneys circulates in the bloodstream and tells the bone marrow to make more blood cells.[3]

When a cell divides, it makes two "offspring," or daughter cells. Those two daughter cells then divide into two more daughter cells. Now there are four cells. These four cells each split into two daughter cells. Now there are eight cells. Those eight cells become sixteen cells, and so on. After only ten cell divisions, that first cell has become 1,024 cells. After fifteen cell divisions, that one original cell has turned into 32,768 daughter cells.

When cells overgrow, a tumor forms. Most tumors are made

up of a billion or more cells before they cause any symptoms.[4] A tumor with one million cells is about the size of a pinhead. This is too small for a tumor within the body to be felt or noticed. Once the tumor contains about a billion cells, it is the size of a small grape. Depending on where the tumor is located, then it may be felt. The tumor will contain about one hundred billion cells by the time it is the size of a golf ball.[5] This means that a lot of tumor growth has already taken place by the time a person goes to the doctor. When cells overgrow and form a tumor, it is a **primary tumor**.

Not all tumors are cancerous. Noncancerous tumors are called **benign** (be-NINE), which means mild. But that does not mean that all benign tumors are harmless. A benign brain tumor, for example, may have to be removed because it may have a harmful effect on neighboring brain tissue. In general, though, benign tumors are easier to treat than cancerous ones.

All cancers have one thing in common—they started as one cell that grew and did not stop.

Cancerous tumors are called **malignant** (muh-LIG-nuhnt). The major difference between benign and malignant tumors is their ability to spread to other parts of the body. Benign tumors do not spread; malignant ones do.

The process of spreading from one part of the body to another is called **metastasis** (muh-TAS-tuh-sis). Cancer cells can spread through the bloodstream or the lymphatic system. The lymphatic system consists of a network of thin tubes that run throughout the body along with the blood vessels. A clear liquid, called lymph, circulates around the body's tissues through the tubes of the lymphatic system. One function of the lymphatic system is to produce white blood cells called lymphocytes, which help the body fight off infections caused by bacteria or viruses. For this reason, the lymphatic system is considered part of the body's immune system. It also functions as a drainage system. As blood circulates through the body, fluid leaks out of the blood vessels into the body's tissues. The lymphatic system collects this fluid and returns it to the bloodstream. Otherwise, the body's tissues would swell with excess fluid. When cancer cells metastasize, they move through blood or lymphatic vessels to another part of the body and form tumors there. Tumors that are formed away from the primary tumor site are called **secondary tumors**.

This ability to invade neighboring tissue is unique to cancer cells. They do this by producing chemicals, called enzymes, which can break down the "glue" that holds normal cells together in a particular order.[6] This allows the cancer cells to push their way in between normal cells and into areas where they are not supposed to be.

Sometimes cells of the body's immune system will find and destroy cancerous cells. But other times, these wayward cells slip through the body's defense system. So, the cancer cells grow and, since they do not die, they clump together and form tumors. The earlier cancer is found, the easier it is to treat. Once it has metastasized, treatment is much more difficult.

Cancer is caused by cells that grow out of control. What causes the cells to do this? Cancer cells keep growing, refusing to die when they are supposed to, because they contain a faulty copy of DNA, the genetic guide that tells them how to behave.

DNA Damage

Every cell in every living thing contains instructions that tell it how to grow and live. This information is carried in a large, complex chemical molecule called DNA, or deoxyribonucleic acid. DNA is the genetic blueprint, or recipe, for making all living things. The DNA molecule is found in the central core, or the nucleus, of every cell.

A DNA molecule looks like a long, twisted ladder. Scientists call this shape a double helix. The sides of the ladder are made

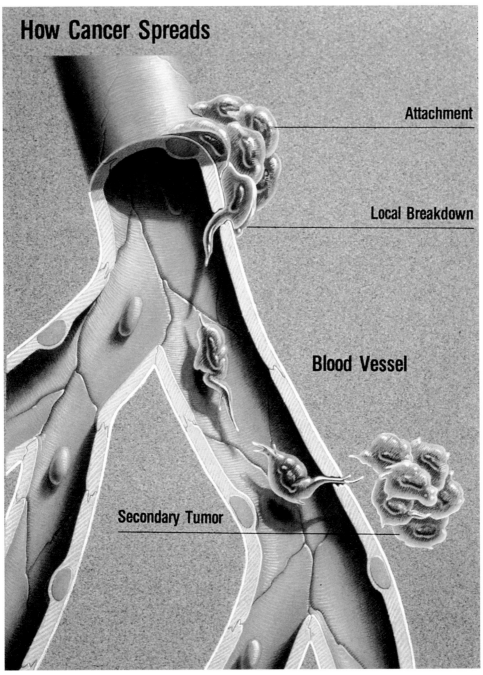

How Cancer Spreads

Attachment

Local Breakdown

Blood Vessel

Secondary Tumor

This diagram shows the process of metastasis, through which cancer cells travel through the bloodstream to other parts of the body and form secondary tumors.

up of a sugar-phosphate "backbone." Sugar groups and phosphate groups alternate over and over to form the sides of the ladder. The rungs of the ladder are made up of four chemicals—adenine (A), cytosine (C), guanine (G), and thymine (T). These four chemicals are called bases and they make up the DNA "alphabet." The DNA alphabet has one major rule: A always pairs with T and C always pairs with G. A DNA molecule is made up of about 3 billion of these base pairs.

During cell division when DNA is copied, the base pairs come apart so there is a single strand of DNA. A single strand of DNA might look like this:

AAGTCATTCCGGAGTCGTCAATAGCTTGCATGTCCA

You can see that the single DNA strand is made up only of letters in the DNA alphabet (A, C, G, and T). In order for the body to "read" the DNA, these letters are grouped together to make up "words." All DNA "words" are three letters long. The sample strand of DNA above would look like this:

AAG TCA TTC CGG AGT CGT CAA TAG CTT GCA TGT CCA

These "words" make up a language that the body's cells can read. The "words" are grouped into "sentences," called **genes**. Genes carry the instructions that tell the body's cells how to make molecules called proteins. Proteins carry out most of the functions the body needs in order to live and grow.

Because the DNA molecule is very long and cells are very small, cells must have a way to store the DNA molecule in a more compact form. To do this, the DNA is wrapped around proteins into a structure called a **chromosome**. Coiled around the proteins like thread around a spool, the DNA does not take up as much space.

Chromosomes, and the genes carried on them, are passed from one generation to the next. You get half your chromosomes from your mother and the other half from your father.

If the entire DNA molecule in the nucleus of one human cell was stretched out it would be almost two meters long. Since the human body contains about five trillion cells, if all of the DNA in an entire human body was stretched out, it would reach from the earth to the sun and back again thirty times![7]

It is possible to inherit a **mutation**, or a mistake, in the DNA from your mother or father.

But mutations are much more likely to happen when the DNA is copied during cell division. Then, newly created DNA is "proofread" by certain molecules. There are checkpoints during each step of DNA **replication**, or copying, and mistakes can be corrected, if needed, at these checkpoints. If mistakes cannot be repaired, however, the cell usually self-destructs. Cancer can develop when there is a problem with either the checkpoints or the self-destruct program. These systems do not work because the DNA has been damaged.

How Does DNA Damage Occur?

There are several ways the DNA molecule can be damaged, causing a mutation. Some DNA damage just naturally builds up as we age. The longer people live, the more times their cells divide. The more cells divide, the more chances there are that the DNA will be copied incorrectly, resulting in DNA damage. That is why almost 77 percent of the people diagnosed with cancer are older than fifty-five.[8]

A chronic illness can be responsible for an abnormal amount of cell death and replacement. People who have a disease called ulcerative colitis, for example, have a higher risk for colon cancer because ulcerative colitis causes an inflammation of the digestive tract. The inflammation causes the cells in the colon to divide rapidly during the healing process. The more the cells divide, the more chances there are for mistakes while the DNA is being copied.

Sometimes, exposure to radiation or certain types of chemicals can cause DNA damage. Not all abnormal cells develop into cancer, however. Most of the time, in fact, they are either found by the body's immune system and destroyed or die on their own. Even if a cell's DNA is mutated, this may not be enough to cause the cell to go into self-destruct mode. The cell may still be able to do its job. Usually it takes more than one mutation in the DNA, or just the right DNA mutation, to produce cancer.

Cancer itself cannot be inherited. But the tendency to develop cancer may be. Certain abnormal genes, the kind that make someone more likely to get cancer, can be passed down from generation to generation. Genes that control cell growth and death are called **proto-oncogenes**. A mutation in a proto-oncogene can lay the groundwork for cancer later in life. A mutated proto-oncogene is called an **oncogene**. Scientists have discovered more than one hundred oncogenes.

Other genes that prevent cells from growing out of control are called **tumor suppressor genes**. When a mutation occurs in a tumor suppressor gene, the cell no longer does its job. The p53 gene is an example of a tumor suppressor gene. Scientists have found that almost 50 percent of tumors have a mutation in the p53 gene. They have found at least fifteen other tumor suppressor genes.[9] Like mutations in oncogenes, mutations in tumor suppressor genes can be passed down from parent to child.

However, even if someone inherits a mutated oncogene or tumor suppressor gene, it does not necessarily mean they will develop cancer. It just means they are predisposed to getting cancer. Being predisposed means that they are more likely to develop cancer than someone who did not inherit a mutated oncogene or tumor suppressor gene. Most DNA mutations are not inherited at all. Instead, they are a result of faulty DNA copying during cell division.

Sometimes DNA damage comes from something outside of the body. There are some substances that we come into contact with every day that are capable of causing cancer. These substances are called **carcinogens** (car-SIN-uh-gins). Tobacco smoke, asbestos, and ultraviolet (UV) radiation are all examples of carcinogens. They can cause cancer in two ways: Either the carcinogen directly damages the DNA or it causes cells to divide more rapidly, possibly leading to more mistakes in copying the DNA.[10]

In most cases, it takes multiple DNA mutations to trigger cancer. This explains why not all smokers get cancer and why not all women who inherit the gene that predisposes them to breast cancer develop the disease.[11] There are a lot of "what ifs" when it comes to determining who might develop the disease.

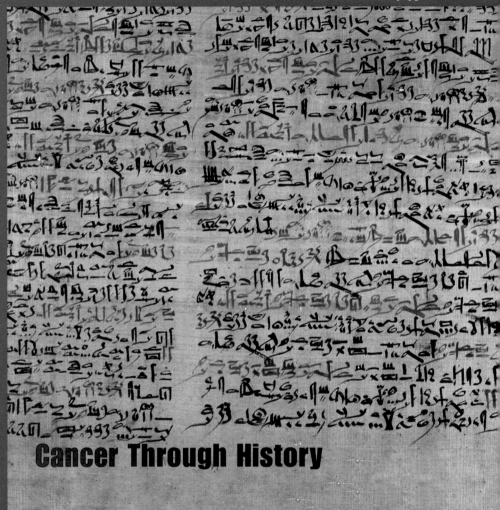

Cancer Through History

It has only been in the last forty years that scientists started to suspect that cancer was caused by damage to DNA.[1] But it is not a new disease. In fact, scientists have found the remains of Egyptian mummies whose bones show signs of osteosarcoma, a type of bone cancer.

Beginning of Cancer

The first known description of cancer is more than 3,500 years old.[2] This document written on papyrus was discovered in 1862, in Luxor, Egypt.[3] The document, called the "Edwin Smith papyrus," in honor of the man who bought and translated it, describes treating tumors with a "fire drill."[4] Scientists believe that this refers to cauterization, destroying abnormal tissue using chemicals or electricity or by heating or freezing cells.[5] Since the ancient Egyptians did not have electricity, the "fire drill" most likely meant using a very hot instrument to destroy abnormal tissue. The Edwin Smith papyrus also discusses surgical treatments of these early cancer cases.

Another document, called the "George Ebers papyrus," discusses medicines and using magic to treat cancer.[6] Scientists believe that the ancient Egyptians may have known the difference between malignant and benign tumors. The ancient doctors may have realized they were not able to cure the disease.[7]

Hippocrates (460–370 B.C.), the Greek physician who is considered the "father of medicine," called the disease *karkinos*, which means "crab" in Greek.[8] Hippocrates probably used this term because the finger-like projections that spread away from a primary tumor look like a crab. The Greek language also gave us another, more technical, term for cancer: neoplasm. *Neo* means "new," and *plasia* means "tissue or cells." So, a neoplasm is a new growth of tissue or cells in the body.

The first known documentation of cancer was written more than 3,500 years ago on a papyrus in Luxor, Egypt.

Early Theories of What Causes Cancer

Humans have tried to find the cause of cancer from the very first instances of the disease. The ancient Egyptians blamed the gods. During the Renaissance Period, scholars like Galileo and Newton investigated phenomena using the scientific method. In medicine, the scientific method opposed the idea that diseases were caused and could be cured by magic, superstition, and religion.[9]

The Scientific Method

The scientific method is used by scientists to gather and test information. Sometimes scientists have questions after they have researched or observed a problem. At other times scientists ask a question first, then research or observe to see if they can find the answer to the question. No matter how they come up with questions, however, scientists will follow the scientific method to find the answers. The steps of the scientific method are:

- Develop a hypothesis. A hypothesis is an educated guess about the answer to a question. A hypothesis is often what is called an if-then statement. For example, a scientist might say "If (I do) this, then (this) will happen."

- Test the hypothesis by doing an experiment.

- Collect and record data. Scientists usually test and gather information several times to make sure the experiment works the same way every time.

- Come to a conclusion. Scientists analyze the data from their experiments to see if the information supports their hypothesis or if it shows that their hypothesis was false.

- Design a new experiment. If their hypothesis is proved false, scientists usually come up with a new hypothesis and experiment again. But even if the experiments show that their hypothesis is true, scientists do not usually stop. Instead, they design a new experiment to test their hypothesis another way.

If repeated experiments show that a hypothesis is true, the hypothesis becomes a scientific theory.

Hippocrates believed that the body was made up of four humors, or bodily fluids—blood, phlegm, yellow bile, and black bile. He thought that a buildup of black bile caused cancer. This theory persisted through the sixteenth century when Gaspare Aselli (1581–1625), an Italian physician, discovered

A sculpture of Hippocrates, the Greek physician known as "the father of medicine." He called the disease *karkinos*, which means "crab" in Greek.

the lymphatic system.[10] Aselli's discovery led doctors at the time to discard the black bile theory of cancer and promoted the idea that abnormalities in the lymphatic system were the true cause of the disease.[11]

Other physicians rejected Aselli's idea. For example, French physician Claude Gendron (1663–1750) thought that cancers did not circulate through the lymphatic system, but instead were hard, localized masses. Gendron did not believe that masses could be treated with medicines, but that they had to be surgically removed along with all of what he called the mass's "filaments."[12]

In the eighteenth century, several factors advanced the knowledge of what caused cancer. In 1761, Giovanni Morgagni (1682–1771) furthered the use of the scientific method in medicine when he became the first doctor to do autopsies, the dissection of a dead body to gain information. He performed more than seven hundred autopsies in an attempt to correlate a patient's illness with what was going on inside the body at the time of death.[13]

That same year, John Hill (1714–1775) was the first person to link tobacco use with cancer. In 1776, Percivall Pott (1714–1788) of London described the first known occupational cause of cancer. Pott discovered that chimney sweeps were at a higher risk of developing cancer due to their exposure to soot.[14] The first hospital specifically devoted to the treatment of cancer opened in 1779 in Reims, France. Doctors believed then that cancer was contagious, so the hospital was located away from the city.[15]

With the invention of the modern microscope in the nineteenth century, Johannes Muller (1801–1858) was able to show that cancerous tumors were made up of cells, not lymph. Muller did not believe, however, that cancer cells came from normal cells. He believed the cancerous cells came from what he called blastemas, or budding elements, that existed between the body's tissues.[16]

The blastema theory lasted until Rudolf Virchow (1821–1902), a German physician and a student of Johannes Muller's, determined that all cells, including cancerous ones, come from other cells. Virchow is often called the father of cellular pathology, the study of abnormalities in cells that are caused by disease. A microscopic view of cancer cells allowed Virchow to diagnose the specific type of cancer and how far advanced it was.[17] This is considered the beginning of scientific **oncology**, the study of cancer.

The Genetic Basis of Cancer

In 1890, just a few years after the discovery of chromosomes, David von Hansemann (1858–1920) first described how cells divided in thirteen different carcinoma samples. A carcinoma is a type of cancer that arises from epithelial cells. These are found in skin, the coverings of all of the body's organs, and the lining of all of its cavities, such as the mouth. Between 80 and 90 percent of all cancers are carcinomas. Not only are they are the most common kind of cancer, there are also many different types of carcinomas. Von Hansemann discovered that the carcinoma cells did not divide the same way normal cells do. He hypothesized that the abnormal division might be the cause of the abnormal number of chromosomes found in some cancer cells.[18]

Other scientists later would learn that cancer arises because of DNA damage. In 1960, scientists found the first chromosomal abnormality linked to a specific type of cancer, chronic myelogenous leukemia (CML).

Researchers Peter Nowell and David Hungerford from the University of Pennsylvania reported that in patients diagnosed with CML, one of the four smallest chromosomes, chromosome 22, was replaced with what they called a "minute chromosome." For many years, scientists thought that the minute chromosome formed when chromosome 22 was deleted. A deleted chromosome is one that has lost some of its genetic material. The loss of DNA material from a chromosome is usually the result of abnormal cell division.

Then, in the early 1970s, scientists discovered better ways to stain chromosomes so they were easier to see and analyze under a microscope. Using the new staining techniques, scientist Janet Rowley determined that the minute chromosome was not actually deleted. Instead, the minute chromosome was formed when part of chromosome 22 broke off and got "stuck" onto another chromosome. This exchange of chromosomal material is called a translocation. In patients with CML, a large part of chromosome 22 breaks off and is translocated onto the bottom of chromosome 9. In addition, a tiny bit of chromosome 9 breaks off and sticks to the bottom of chromosome 22. The name

A lithograph showing an English chimney sweep, made about 1875. It was discovered that sweepers were more prone to develop cancer because of their exposure to soot.

Leukemia and Lymphoma

Leukemia is the general name used for four different types of blood cancers: acute myelogenous leukemia (AML), chronic myelogenous leukemia (CML), acute lymphocytic leukemia (ALL), and chronic lymphocytic leukemia (CLL). All four of these cancers start with one abnormal bone marrow cell that grows out of control. Bone marrow is the spongy tissue at the center of bones that is responsible for making red blood cells, white blood cells, and platelets. AML and CML begin as abnormal stem cells in the bone marrow. Stem cells are immature cells that have not yet turned into red blood cells, white blood cells, or platelets. Some bone marrow stem cells develop into certain types of white blood cells called lymphocytes. If one of these lymphocytes, which are a part of the immune system, turns cancerous, ALL and CLL are the result.

Without treatment, the acute leukemias progress very quickly. Abnormal leukemia cells grow quickly and live longer than normal blood cells, but they do not work the way normal blood cells do. When too many leukemia cells accumulate in the bone marrow, they prevent the bone marrow from functioning as it should. Chronic leukemias progress slower than acute leukemias. These abnormal leukemia cells do not accumulate in the bone marrow as quickly and the bone marrow is still able to make normal cells.

Lymphoma is the term used for cancers of the lymphatic system. These cancers usually begin in a lymph node or lymphatic tissue in organs such as the spleen or intestines.

of the minute chromosome was eventually changed to the "Philadelphia chromosome," named for the city where it was discovered. Rowley went on to discover several more translocations that are specific to other types of cancer.

In 1982, scientists discovered why these rearrangements in the chromosomes caused cancer. They found that when part of chromosome 9 is transferred to chromosome 22, a gene called c-ABL moved with it. About the same time that scientists discovered c-ABL, other scientists found that a gene called c-MYC was disrupted during the translocation between chromosome 8 and 14. This translocation has been associated with Burkitt lymphoma.[19] In their normal state, c-ABL and ac-MYC are proto-oncogenes. When they are moved and/or disrupted, the cells containing the mutated genes lose control of how many times the cell can divide and grow. The mutated genes are now called oncogenes. Oncogenes are capable of transforming normal cells into cancerous ones by allowing overgrowth or sometimes even promoting it.

Scientists called **cytogenetiscists** can determine what type of leukemia or lymphoma someone has based on the chromosomal anomalies. They also monitor the number of abnormal cells seen throughout treatment—the fewer abnormal cells, the better the treatment is working. Today, the study of chromosomes is still the most reliable way to diagnose and to monitor leukemia and lymphomas.[20]

History of Cancer Research and Treatment

In the 1700s, John Hunter (1728–1793), a Scottish surgeon, suggested that some cancers could be treated with surgery.

Wilhelm Conrad Roentgen (1845–1923) discovered X-rays in 1896. And, by 1899, they were being used as a radiation treatment for cancer.[21] In 1946, Louis Goodman (1906–2000) realized that mustard gas had the potential to be used as the first chemotherapy drug.[22] Mustard gas was used as a chemical weapon in World War I, when military doctors noticed that soldiers exposed to the gas had very low white blood cell counts.[23] Doctors thought that if the mustard gas killed rapidly dividing white blood cells, maybe it would do the same thing to cancer cells. In the 1940s, several patients with advanced lymphoma were given a liquid form of mustard gas. The drug worked, at least for a while. This led doctors to look for other drugs that would kill cancer cells.[24]

Prior to this discovery, another research advance came in 1915, when scientists at Tokyo University succeeded in causing

How Cells Package Genetic Information

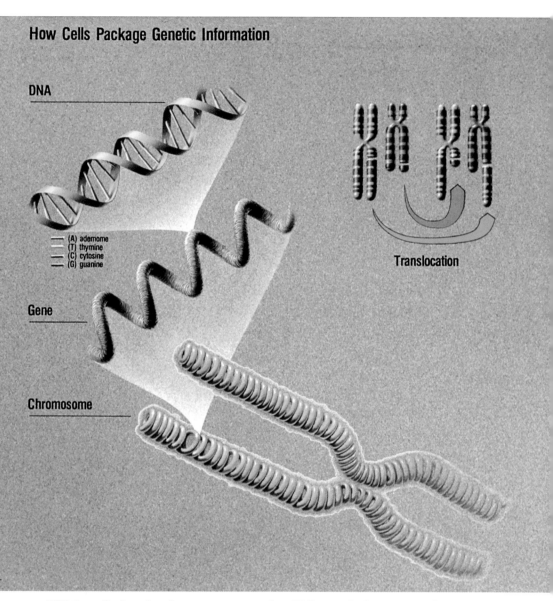

DNA

- (A) adenome
- (T) thymine
- (C) cytosine
- (G) guanine

Gene

Chromosome

Translocation

DNA is coiled up in chromosomes so it will fit neatly into a cell. Genes are particular sections of a chromosome that code for one particular protein. The process of translocation is one way in which DNA can be mutated.

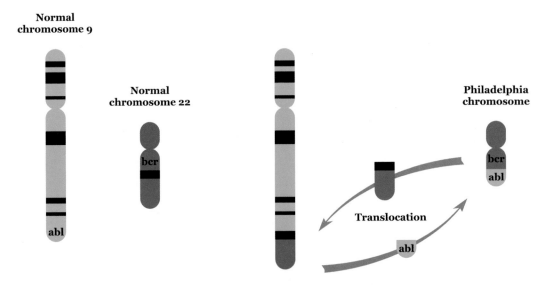

Normal chromosome 9

Normal chromosome 22

bcr

abl

Philadelphia chromosome

bcr

abl

Translocation

abl

As shown in this diagram, the translocation between chromosome 9 and chromosome 22 causes chronic myelogenous leukemia, because the *abl* and *bcr* genes are disrupted.

cancer deliberately in a laboratory rabbit by putting coal tar onto its skin.[25] This was an important step because scientists today use animals to provide a model for human cancers. This allows scientists to study suspected carcinogens without exposing humans to them. Animals are used to test new treatments and their side effects before human trials are attempted.

Types of Cancer

Cancers are usually named for the organ in which they originate. Lung cancer, for example, starts in the lungs, and it is still called lung cancer even if it has metastasized and moved to other areas of the body.

Doctors also classify cancers based on what types of cells they come from—epithelial cells, connective tissue cells, blood-forming cells, and nerve cells. Epithelial cells are found in skin, the coverings of all of the body's organs, and the lining of all of

Five Major Groups of Cancers

1. **Carcinomas—Formed from epithelial cells; can be further subdivided into adenocarcinomas and squamous cell carcinomas.**

    a. **adenocarcinomas—Develop in cells lining a gland or the ducts of a gland. Some types of cancer that form in the breast, prostate, salivary glands, pancreas, and endocrine glands are a few examples of adenocarcinomas.**[26]

    b. **squamous cell carcinomas—Found in the linings of organs, capillaries, or the alveoli of the lungs.**[27]

2. **Sarcomas—Arise from connective tissue cells. Osteosarcoma, for example, is a sarcoma that originates in the bones.**

3. **Myelomas—Form in the plasma cells. Plasma cells make some of the proteins found in the blood or bone marrow.**

4. **Leukemias—Form in the bone marrow.**

5. **Lymphomas—Form in a part of the lymphatic system.**

its cavities, such as the mouth. Connective tissue cells include bones, muscles, tendons, cartilage, and blood vessels. The bone marrow contains blood-forming cells. Nerve cells are found all over the body, including the brain.

Cancers that begin in a particular organ can sometimes be subdivided by the type of cells they come from, too. Skin cancer, for example, can be subdivided into three different types of skin cancer: basal cell, squamous cell, and melanoma. Melanoma, the most dangerous type of skin cancer, arises from melanocytes, or pigment cells, in the deepest layer of skin. Melanoma is so dangerous because it can metastasize very quickly, which makes it hard to cure. Melanoma can show up almost anywhere on the body, even places that are not regularly exposed to the sun, like the soles of the feet or between the toes. Basal and squamous cell skin cancers, on the other hand, are curable. These two types of skin cancer usually arise in areas that are often exposed to sun, like the face, hands, and ears.

NERAL'S WARNING: Smoking Causes Lung Cancer se, Emphysema, And May Complicate Pregnancy.

Risky Business

Risk factors are activities or circumstances that increase the chance of developing cancer. Some risk factors can be changed or avoided, but others cannot. Because all people have a unique genetic makeup, determining cancer risk is a very individual process. And, while people cannot control some risk factors such as family history, age, and ethnicity, others such as whether or not they smoke and the types and quantity of food they eat are controllable. Even if people have one or more cancer risk factors, this does not necessarily mean that they will get cancer. And even if they do, there is no way to prove that the risk factor was what caused the cancer. Some people who develop cancer do not appear to have any risk factors at all while others have many risk factors and never develop the disease.

The search for an actual "cause" of cancer has been going on for centuries. Along the way, scientists have come to several faulty conclusions, such as all cancer is a natural aging process, or that all cancer is caused by "irritants" such as smoke or coal tar, or that it is caused by viruses or bacteria, or passed down in families. While some of these things have been proven to be true in the case of *some* cancers, scientists have found that there is no one central cause for all DNA damage. Not all older people get cancer. Not everyone who smokes or has a family history of cancer develops the disease.[1] But all these things are considered risk factors. Doctors sometimes say that having a family history of cancer or being exposed to certain chemicals predisposes someone to developing cancer. A predisposition means someone may be more likely to get the disease than someone who is not exposed to certain chemicals or who has no family history of the disease.

Smoking and Other Tobacco Use

Cigarette smoking is linked to about one third of all the cancer deaths in the United States each year.[2] It is the leading cause of lung cancer in both men and women. It does not just cause lung cancer. Cigarettes and other tobacco products such as cigars, chewing tobacco, and snuff have also been determined to be the main cause of cancers of the larynx, esophagus, and mouth. They have also been linked to cancers of the bladder, kidney, pancreas, and cervix.[3] The risk is so high because tobacco, and its smoke, is full of chemicals. In fact, it contains more than sixty carcinogens.[4]

Scientists know this because they have conducted laboratory and epidemiological studies on tobacco use. Laboratory studies can involve cells in a petri dish and/or laboratory animals, such as mice, being exposed to the potential carcinogen. Since there are far too many chemicals, both natural and man-made, to test all of them this way, scientists pick only certain ones. They test any chemical that humans are likely to come into contact with in quantities that might cause them harm. They also look at ones that have similar chemical structures to other substances already known to cause cancer, and substances that other lab tests have shown to be suspect.

Laboratory animals exposed to suspected carcinogens are called animal models. Animal models are designed to mimic what would happen in a human if they were exposed to the chemical. Mice make good animal models because they have a short life span. This means that the scientists can see whether or not cancer will develop in a matter of months instead of the years that it would take to develop in humans. Most of the time, the animal models are exposed to large amounts of the suspected carcinogen, much more than most people would be exposed to in their everyday lives. Scientists do this so that the fewest animals are used. They assume that if a large amount of a chemical causes cancer in the animals, it will eventually cause cancer in humans, too. However, substances that cause cancer in mice do not always cause cancer in humans.

The other type of study done by scientists to link certain chemicals with cancer is called an epidemiological study. These types of studies look at a group of people who have already developed a certain type of cancer. Scientists then try to determine which factors might be linked to that type of cancer. One problem with epidemiological studies is that people do not live in a controlled environment. They are constantly exposed to all types of chemicals, not just the one that the scientists are testing. Another problem is that it often takes years, sometimes even decades, before humans exposed to a carcinogen develop cancer. For this reason, it can be very hard to know for sure which chemicals or exposures might have led to the disease.[5]

After many studies, though, scientists have no doubt that

Three types of lab mice used in experiments. Mice are good animal models because scientists can expose them to suspected carcinogens and find out what happens in a short period of time.

tobacco and its smoke are carcinogens. Research has shown that because tobacco smoke is inhaled, it increases a person's risk of getting lung and mouth cancers, cancer of the pharynx (which is behind the nose), and cancer of the larynx (voice box). Cancers of the esophagus and stomach are linked to tobacco smoke because it is swallowed. Because some of the carcinogens from the smoke can enter the blood stream and circulate throughout the body, smoking is also linked to cancers of the pancreas, liver, and cervix. And, finally, because these carcinogens have to be filtered from the blood into the urine, smoking also increases the chances of developing kidney and bladder cancers.[6]

Snuff and chewing tobacco, also called smokeless tobacco, can be equally harmful. Smokeless tobacco contains twenty-eight known carcinogens and can increase a person's risk of developing cancers of the lip, tongue, cheeks, gums, and the floor or the roof of the mouth.[7]

The younger someone starts using tobacco products and the longer they continue, the more likely they are to develop cancer. People who smoke tobacco products are not putting only their own lives at risk. Anyone inhaling their tobacco smoke is at higher risk for developing lung cancer, too. Secondhand smoke causes more than three thousand lung cancer deaths in nonsmokers every year.[8]

Food

Scientific evidence also shows that about one third of the cancer deaths in the United States each year are related to food choices. High-fat diets have been linked to cancers of the prostate, colon, and rectum. Scientists believe that one possible explanation is that excess fat in the diet seems to increase the production of **free radicals**. Free radicals are chemicals that react very easily with other chemicals in the body. When free radicals react with some body chemicals, they can cause biological damage. They are linked to many different types of cancers.[9]

Research has also shown that certain chemicals added to food to help preserve it and certain cooking methods may also increase cancer risk. Nitrates, which are used in pickling food, and other chemicals used to smoke food seem to increase the risk of stomach cancer. Pickling, curing, and smoking meats were used to preserve food before refrigeration. Studies have shown that modern refrigeration has decreased the number of digestive system cancers, probably by eliminating some of the chemicals used in these processes.[10] Pickling food also seems to increase the risk of developing cancer of the esophagus or stomach, especially if the

Cigarette smoking is linked to about one third of all the cancer deaths in the United States each year.

food is salty. Scientists think the popularity of pickled food in Japan may explain why that country has such high rates of esophageal and stomach cancers.[11]

Most food additives do not seem to affect cancer risk one way or the other. Scientists constantly test the colorings, flavoring, and sweeteners that go into our food. If they posed a major risk to most people, these things would be removed from the market. Sometimes, though, these additives can be involved in what is called a "cancer scare." Saccharin is a good example of this. Scientists found that rats given massive amounts of saccharin had a higher incidence of cancer. Many foods and drinks containing saccharin were pulled off of the grocery shelf. But it is unlikely that humans would ever consume the massive amounts of saccharin that the rats were given. The U.S. Food and Drug Administration (FDA) removed saccharin from their list of suspected carcinogens in the year 2000.[12]

Sometimes it is not what is added to the food that might increase cancer risk but how it is cooked. For example, the smoke caused by fat dripping from meat onto a hot grill deposits chemicals onto the meat. Scientists know that these chemicals cause cancer in laboratory animals. Grilling fruits and vegetables poses no risk because they contain no fat. When food is charred, or blackened, like when it is broiled, for example, another type of chemical is formed in the food. These chemicals are also suspected to cause cancer. So, theoretically, cooking food in these ways may increase your risk of developing cancer. However, there have been no scientific studies so far that have shown this happening in humans.[13] Just in case, scientists recommend using leaner cuts of meat on the grill to prevent fats from dripping onto the heat source. They also suggest cooking food without burning, or charring, it to prevent these chemicals from forming.[14]

So far, scientists say that there is no real scientific evidence that points to a need for changing cooking and eating habits for the general public in the hopes of decreasing cancer risks.[15] However, eating leaner meat, less fat, and more whole grains, fruits, and vegetables is part of a healthy, balanced diet.

Fun in the Sun

It may be fun to go to the beach, but it is not so much fun to get sunburned. In fact, it could be downright dangerous. Doctors say about 65 percent of melanomas and 90 percent of basal and squamous cell skin cancers come from exposure to ultraviolet (UV) rays from the sun.[16] The risk of developing skin cancer increases if a person is light skinned, has a lot of moles, or has had a relative who has had melanoma skin cancer.

Non-melanoma skin cancer is thought to be caused by long-term exposure to the sun over a lifetime. But melanoma, the most dangerous type of skin cancer, is believed to be caused by short periods of intense exposure that lead to very bad sunburns. This seems to be true especially if the bad sunburns happen during childhood. Research has shown that people who

Certain methods of cooking meat are suspected to pose a cancer risk.

suffer bad sunburns in childhood are much more likely to develop melanoma later in life.[17]

Physicists classify ultraviolet rays into three categories depending on their wavelengths—UVA has the longest wavelength, UVC has the shortest, and UVB has a wavelength in between the other two types. The shorter the wavelength, the more energy the UV light has and the more damage it can do to DNA. Fortunately, UVC—the most energetic of the ultraviolet rays—is completely absorbed by the gases in Earth's atmosphere and never reaches the ground. This is good, because any exposure to UVC can destroy skin![18]

Exposure to Radiation

UV rays are a source of radiation that we are exposed to every day. Radiation is the release of energy from any source. UV rays

Protect Yourself

UVA and UVB, with their longer wavelengths, can pass right through Earth's atmosphere. Sunscreens either absorb UVB rays before they get to the skin or they reflect the solar rays away from the skin. Many sunscreens do not absorb or reflect the longer wavelength of the UVA rays, though.[19] The ones that do are called broad-spectrum sunscreens.

The beach is not the only place people are exposed to UV rays. Tanning beds and sun lamps emit UVA and UVB rays, too. Many tanning parlors claim that tanning beds are safe because they emit mostly UVA rays. But UVA rays have been linked with malignant melanoma. The Federal Drug Administration (FDA) and the Centers for Disease Control (CDC) urge people not to use tanning beds and to take precautions to limit sun exposure when they are outside. Their recommendations include wearing a broad-spectrum sunscreen (one that blocks both UVA and UVB solar rays) with a sun protection factor (SPF) of at least 15, sunglasses that provide 100-percent UV protection, and a broad-brimmed hat to keep the sun off of your face.

and radon gas are natural sources of radiation that people are exposed to throughout their lifetimes. Radon gas is a natural radioactive gas found in rocks, soil, and water. You cannot see, taste, or smell radon. But it is the second-leading cause of lung cancer, after smoking, and it is the leading cause of lung cancer in nonsmokers.[20] There are other sources of radiation which are not natural. These include atomic bombs or nuclear power plant disasters such as the nuclear reactor accident in Chernobyl, Ukraine, on April 26, 1986.

Radiation can be divided into two different types—ionizing radiation and nonionizing radiation. Exposure to ionizing radiation can cause cancer by damaging DNA. Nonionizing radiation does not have as much energy as ionizing radiation. The only source of nonionizing radiation linked to cancer so far is UV rays from the sun. Other sources of nonionizing radiation include microwave ovens, electromagnetic fields, radio waves, and radiation given off by household electrical appliances, heaters, cell phones, and computers and their screens. There have been studies to determine if electromagnetic fields (like those given off by overhead power lines) cell phones, or computers can cause cancer. So far, there is no scientific evidence to show that any of these things do, but research continues.[21] Not everyone exposed to radiation will get cancer, but it is thought that the more exposure you get, the more susceptible you are.[22]

Family History

Cancer, by definition, means that the DNA in some cells is defective. The abnormality may be inherited, meaning that it was passed from parent to child through the chromosomes. Or damage to the DNA could be due to exposure to carcinogens and happen later in life.

Some common cancers, such as breast, colon, ovarian, and uterine cancers, occur in some families generation after generation. In fact, breast cancer, one type of colon cancer, and an eye cancer called retinoblastoma have all been linked to specific genes that can be passed down from parent to child.[23] The genes that are associated with an increased risk of developing breast cancer are called BRCA1 and BRCA2. Women who inherit one of these defective genes have a higher risk of developing breast cancer. But most women who get breast cancer do not have either of these genes. In fact, women who carry these genes account for less than 5 percent of all breast cancer cases.[24]

Certain genetic disorders can increase a person's risk of developing cancer, too. Genetic disorders are caused by missing, additional, or mutated chromosomes and are present at birth. People born with Down syndrome, for example, have an extra copy of chromosome 21. For reasons that doctors still do not understand, people born with Down syndrome are more likely than the general population to develop childhood leukemia, but they are less likely to get other forms of cancer.[25] Fanconi anemia, a rare disorder of the blood and bone marrow that affects children, is not a cancer, but it seems to increase the risk of developing leukemia, a bone marrow cancer.[26] Most scientists, however, believe that while there is a genetic link to some forms of cancer, lifestyle choices and environmental exposure to carcinogens are responsible for many more cancers than is family history.

The Workplace

Working with asbestos, a material once used to insulate buildings and help make them fireproof, can cause a type of lung cancer called mesothelioma. The lung cancer does not develop right away. Instead, it may take twenty to thirty years to develop.[27] Because of its link to cancer, the Environmental Protection Agency (EPA) has banned many of the uses for asbestos. Today it is usually only found in older buildings. Benzene is another chemical people could be exposed to at work

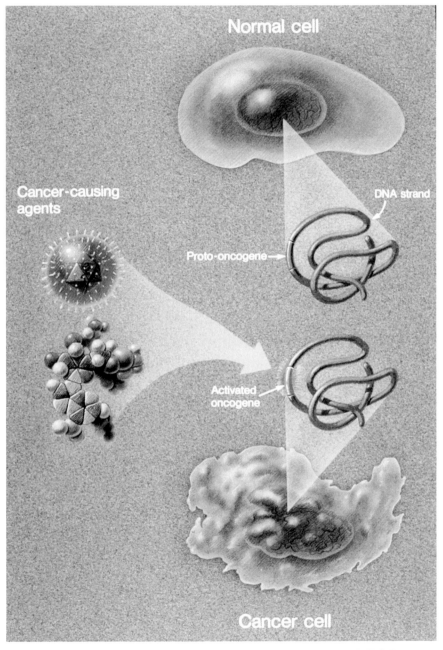

A proto-oncogene in a normal cell controls cell growth and division. When a carcinogen affects a cell's DNA, the proto-oncogene can mutate into an oncogene, causing the cell to turn cancerous, as shown in this diagram.

that increases their risk of developing cancer. Benzene is a sweet smelling, colorless liquid that is used in the rubber industry, oil refineries, chemical plants, shoe manufacturing, and gasoline-related industries. Workers who use or make this chemical at work could be at a higher risk of developing acute myeloid leukemia (AML) or, less frequently, chronic lymphocytic leukemia (CLL). Benzene is also found in cigarette smoke.[28]

Microorganisms: Viruses and Bacteria

Viruses can invade cells and change their genetic makeup. The Epstein-Barr virus (EBV), for example, is linked to a type of lymphoma found mostly in children from sub-Saharan Africa.[29] A lot of people have been exposed and infected with EBV because it is the same virus that causes mononucleosis, or "mono." Yet, not everyone infected with EBV develops cancer. Scientists believe that infection with EBV along with repeated bouts of malaria may be what causes lymphoma.

The hepatitis B and C viruses have also been linked with cancer. Hepatitis attacks the liver and is responsible for many cases of liver cancer around the world. China, Taiwan, Japan, and Thailand have the highest number of people infected with the hepatitis B virus. They also have the highest rate of liver cancer.

Scientists believe that viruses may promote cancer in one of two ways. The virus could contain an oncogene (a gene that promotes cell growth), or the virus may insert its DNA into the host's DNA in such a way that damages a gene designed to control cell growth.[30]

Viruses are not the only microorganisms linked to cancer. Scientists think that long-term infection with the bacteria *Helicobacter pylori* (known as *H. pylori*), the same type of bacteria that is responsible for stomach ulcers, might eventually lead to stomach cancer. They believe this is due to increased cell division that is required to repair damage done to the stomach by the constant irritation. More than half of stomach cancer cases have been linked to *H. pylori* infection. But not everyone who is infected with the bacteria gets cancer.[31]

Weakened Immune System

People with a weakened immune system may also be at a higher risk for developing certain types of cancer. A weakened immune system is one that does not function properly. This includes people who have had organ transplants, because they are on immune-suppressing drugs to keep their immune systems from rejecting their new organs; people who are infected with the HIV/AIDS virus; or people who are born with rare birth defects that affect their immune system. Scientists believe that a weakened immune system can put these people at risk in several different ways. Because their immune system does not work the way it should, patients with weakened immune systems are more likely to be infected with viruses and bacteria, such as hepatitis or *H. pylori*. Repeated infections may also stimulate the immune system to produce more cells to fight off the infections. Because of the rapid cell division, the DNA in these immune cells could be copied incorrectly leading to lymphoma.[32]

This is why cancer is often called a multifactorial disease. Multifactorial means there are many factors involved. No single factor causes cancer. Most types of cancer are more common as we get older, because it takes time for DNA damage to accumulate. But getting older is not the only factor at work.

Preventive Measures

Sometimes it is hard to separate what scientists and doctors already know about cancer from what is still under investigation. Newspaper headlines and advertisements might claim that a new cancer cause, prevention, or cure has been discovered. Some of these reports might be accurate but others may stem from only one study or studies done only in mice. A few of these claims may have not been studied scientifically at all. While every scientific effort in the search for cancer cures and preventions is important, it takes many studies to actually prove that a nutrient, supplement, drug, or other method prevents or treats cancer. Furthermore, what works in mice does not always work in humans. However, there are some ways—such as getting early screenings for some cancers, eating a healthy diet, not smoking, getting enough exercise, and maintaining a healthy weight—to protect some people against the likelihood of getting cancer.

Screening Tests

Screening tests are done on healthy people with no symptoms of cancer solely for the purpose of trying to find certain cancers early. These screening tests are usually performed as part of a routine, yearly checkup. They are one reason why doctors recommend that people see their physician once a year. One screening test used since the 1900s, the Papanicolaou smear (Pap smear) is a routine test for cervical cancer. This test can detect abnormal cells when there are only a few present. At a routine checkup, a doctor might also order a blood test to screen for prostate cancer in men or a mammogram, a special type of X-ray, to check for breast cancer in women.

An abnormal screening test result does not automatically mean that someone has cancer. Sometimes it just means that abnormal cells are present. These abnormal cells may turn cancerous someday. Or they may not. In these cases, a doctor might recommend that the person get follow-up screening tests more frequently. This is to make sure that the abnormal cells are not changing. At other times, a screening test may indicate that cancerous cells are already present and that further testing needs to be done.

Screening tests are not available for all types of cancer, and they do not always detect cancer in the earliest stages. But screening tests may help catch the presence of cancerous cells early. That is when there is the best chance for successful treatment.

Lifestyle Risk Factors

There are some ways people can live that may protect them from developing cancer later in life. For example, doctors recommend avoiding known carcinogens, such as cigarette smoke and excessive sun exposure. The easiest way to prevent cancers linked to tobacco is to not smoke cigarettes, cigars, or pipes, and to not use smokeless tobacco. If you do not smoke now, do not start. If a loved one smokes, ask the person to quit. It is not easy to stop smoking once you have started, but it may save lives in the long run. Also try to avoid breathing in other people's smoke. Secondhand smoke is harmful, too.

Another risky behavior that can be controlled is exposure to the sun. Nobody can completely avoid being in the sun, so protect against skin cancer by using a sunscreen or sun block with a SPF of at least 15. Reapply the sunscreen every two hours and do not get sunburned. Between 11:00 A.M. and 3:00 P.M., when the sun's rays are strongest, either stay out of the sun or wear long sleeves, long pants, and a hat.

Melanoma, the most dangerous form of skin cancer, can sometimes be confused with a regular mole. But life-threatening melanomas can be detected using the "ABCD" rule. "A" stands for **asymmetry**. Most moles are symmetrical, meaning that if you were to draw a line down the middle of the mole, the two halves would look like mirror images of one another. Melanomas are asymmetrical—their two halves look different. "B" stands for **border**. Melanomas do not have a distinct border around them. The border between normal skin and a melanoma may be notched or jagged. "C" stands for **color**. Most moles are all one color, either all light or all dark. But melanomas often have different colors in them. And "D" stands for **diameter**, or how big the

Screening tests may help catch the presence of cancerous cells early. That is when there is the best chance for successful treatment.

Shown is a melanoma with a ragged border. Use the ABCDs to determine whether a suspicious mole is really melanoma; when in doubt, consult a doctor.

spot is. If a suspicious-looking mole is bigger than the size of a pencil eraser (about six millimeters wide), it should be checked by a doctor.[1]

Can the Food You Eat Protect You From Cancer?

There is debate about whether eating or not eating certain foods can reduce the risk of developing cancer. Some of the foods that seem to have a protective effect are fruits and vegetables, certain types of oils found in fish, foods with lots of fiber, and vitamins A, C, E, and D. People take vitamin A, C, E, or D supplements, believing that this might help protect them from developing cancer. But it does not seem to work that way. Scientists have found that there is something about eating foods rich in these vitamins that may have a protective effect. Taking vitamin supplements, on the other hand, does not seem to work as well.[2]

Nutritionists think the type of diet that lowers the risk of developing cancer is basically the same diet recommended to keep your heart healthy. And while it may eventually turn out that these measures do not affect cancer risk one way or the other, eating a healthy, well-balanced diet cannot hurt. A healthy diet includes eating less red meat and animal fat (butter, cheese, ice cream), getting at least five servings of fruits or vegetables every day, eating more fish, increasing the amount of fiber and whole grains, and eating less salt and sugar.

Fruits, vegetables, beans, whole grains, and other foods derived from plants contain chemicals called **phytochemicals** that may help fight cancer. There are thousands of phytochemcials, which are also sometimes called antioxidants, flavonoids, or isoflavones. Scientists have only studied a few of these in depth, including beta carotene, ascorbic acid (vitamin C), folic acid, and vitamin E.[3] Some scientific studies have shown evidence that eating foods rich in these nutrients may protect some people from developing certain cancers, but more research is needed.

Above all, people should try to avoid behaviors such as smoking and excessive sun exposure that scientists know are linked to increased cancer risk. Eating a well-balanced, healthy diet and maintaining a healthy weight may help reduce cancer risk, too. Being overweight has been linked to several different types of cancer including colon, breast, and uterine cancer.[4] Eating a healthy diet and getting enough exercise are the keys to preventing all kinds of diseases, including cancer.

Nutritionists believe that a healthy diet with an emphasis on whole grains, fruits, and vegetables can help prevent cancer.

Vaccines

Scientists are also working on vaccines that could protect people from developing cancer. Right now, there are two types of cancer vaccines—therapeutic and prophylactic. Therapeutic vaccines are designed to stimulate the immune system into recognizing cancer cells as cells that need to be destroyed. At present, therapeutic vaccines are experimental and are being tested in a relatively small number of cancer patients.

The other type of vaccine, called a prophylactic, or preventive, vaccine, is designed to stop cancer from forming by preventing a viral infection. So far, the FDA has approved two prophylactic vaccines. One is to prevent infection with the hepatitis B virus, which is linked to liver cancer. The other, more recent, vaccine is Gardasil, which lowers the risk of cervical cancer by preventing infection by certain strains of the human papillomavirus (HPV).[5] The four strains of HPV that the vaccine protects against are thought to cause up to 70 percent of cervical cancer cases.[6]

Though men can also get HPV, cervical cancer occurs only in women. So, Gardasil is recommended only for girls and women nine to twenty-six years of age. This is because the vaccine works best if a woman has never been exposed to HPV, which is a sexually transmitted virus. Therefore, the FDA recommends that females get vaccinated before becoming sexually active. Scientists are still studying the drug to see if it may also protect women over the age of twenty-six. Because Gardasil does not prevent infection with all strains of HPV, it will not prevent all cases of cervical cancer, but it does lower the risk of developing the disease.

Ultimately, scientists do not know why certain people get cancer while others do not. Some people can do everything they can to reduce their risk factors and still develop the disease, while others may do nothing at all and never develop cancer. Apparently, much depends on a person's genetic makeup.

Diagnosis 5

Cancer can begin in any part of the body except the teeth, hair, and fingernails. In order to treat cancer effectively, doctors need to find where the cancer started and how far it has spread. But diagnosing cancer is not easy. Many of the early symptoms of cancer can be the same as the symptoms of a much less serious disease. For example, blood in the urine could be caused by kidney cancer, but it could also be a kidney infection. Weight loss and stomach pain could be due to an ulcer, or it could be stomach cancer. People also tend to think of many of these symptoms as not severe enough to see a doctor about or as something that will go away on their own. That may not be true, so it is better to check with a doctor.

Biopsy

If a doctor does suspect cancer, the patient may need a **biopsy**. During a biopsy, a doctor will take a small sample of tissue from the suspicious area. This can be done by surgically removing all, or part, of a tumor. Or it can be done with a needle inserted into the tumor, which draws out some tumor cells. This is called a needle biopsy. A pathologist, a doctor who specializes in analyzing tissue, then examines the sample under a microscope to determine if cancer cells are present. Only a small amount of tissue is needed, just enough for a pathologist to see if the cells are cancerous.

Staging

Different patients with the same type of cancer can have very different long-term outcomes, even if their cancers are treated in the same way. Therefore, one of the most important things the oncologist will do is try to accurately "stage" the patient. Cancer staging systems describe the location of the primary tumor, how big and how many tumors there are, and whether the cancer has spread or not. Staging will often involve physical exams, X-rays or CT scans, blood tests, and sometimes even surgery.

A doctor is usually most concerned with whether the cancer is present only at the site where it started or whether it has spread to other parts of the body. Each cancer or part of the body may have a different staging system. However, in general, patients with Stage I have local disease that has not spread elsewhere in the body. Stage II means a larger tumor or some spreading of the tumor in the local area. Stage III cancers have usually spread more into the local or regional part of the body,

Who Are These People?

There are many people involved in the diagnosis and treatment of cancer. The main doctor is an oncologist, who specializes in the treatment of cancer. There are many different types of oncologists:

- A medical oncologist is the doctor who prescribes and monitors the effects of chemotherapy, diagnoses and treats complications, and develops a treatment plan for the patient.

- A surgical oncologist removes tumors.

- A pediatric oncologist deals with cancers found in children.

- A radiation oncologist prescribes and monitors radiation treatment of cancer.

- Other types of oncologists may specialize in cancers of a specific organ or bodily system, such as breast, lung, bone, or leukemia.

A cancer patient might encounter other professionals, too:

- Nurses administer any medication an oncologist orders and help the patient prepare for diagnostic testing.

- Pathologists are doctors who identify what type of cancer the patient has and how far it has progressed by looking at a sample of cancer cells removed during surgery. A pathologist can also tell the surgeon if all the cancer has been removed during surgery.

- Radiologists are doctors who specialize in reading and understanding the test results from equipment such as X-ray machines, MRIs, CT scans, ultrasounds, and PET scans, all advanced methods of seeing inside the body.

- Cytogenetiscists are scientists who specialize in studying the chromosomes to look for DNA changes that might cause specific types of cancer.

- Epidemiologists study groups of people looking for evidence of cancer clusters. A cancer cluster is a higher-than-expected number of cancer cases in a certain group of people over a certain period of time. For example, if people in one particular neighborhood develop cancer more often than would normally be expected to occur randomly over a particular time period, an epidemiologist might be called in to see if there are carcinogens present in the neighborhood's environment.

- Technologists and technicians help many of these scientists in the laboratory.

> **Different patients with the same type of cancer can have very different long-term outcomes, even if their cancers are treated in the same way.**

while Stage IV cancers have spread to completely different parts of the body.

Staging helps cancer specialists decide how to treat the patient. Staging information can help decide whether his or her cancer might be cured by surgery alone, which type of surgery might be needed, and what other treatments might be necessary. Staging is also used to predict the outcome, or prognosis, of the patient's cancer, based on what has happened in the past to patients with the same type of cancer found at the same stage.[1] In general, the higher the stage, the more the cancer has spread and the worse the outcome is likely to be.

Imaging Tests

Imaging tests allow doctors to take pictures of what is going on inside the body. All imaging tests pass energy through the body to produce pictures. But each test uses a different type of energy. X-rays can be used as an imaging test for detecting cancer. An X-ray machine produces a beam of radiation, or energy, which passes through the body and lands on a special type of film. Different parts of the body block the X-rays from reaching the film in different amounts. Dense parts, like bones, block much of the X-ray energy and appear almost white on the resulting X-ray film. Other areas of the body, like the lungs, which are mostly air, appear almost black on the film because most of the radiation goes right through them. Other organs appear in different shades of gray. Tumors, which are usually denser than the tissue around them, show up as a lighter shade of gray.[2]

Another type of imaging test, a magnetic resonance imaging (MRI) test, uses a large magnet and radio waves to take pictures

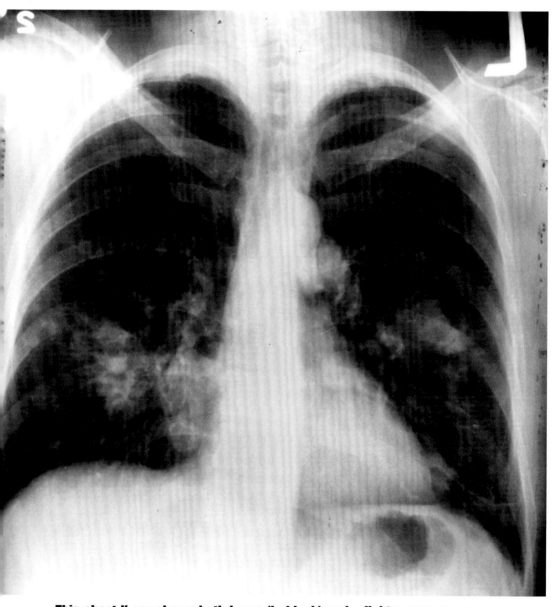

This chest X-ray shows both lungs (in black) and a lighter gray mass that could indicate cancer.

of the inside of the body. The machine is a long tube that patients pass through while lying on a bed. MRIs are painless but very noisy. This type of imaging test can be used on most parts of the body, but it is very sensitive to movement, so it is rarely used for mouth cancers because swallowing can lead to a blurry picture. For some parts of the body, a MRI will give clearer pictures, while for other parts, a CT scan is better.[3]

A CT or CAT scan is a computerized axial tomography scan. During a CT scan, the patient lies motionless on a bed inside a ring of X-ray tubes. During this painless scan, pictures are taken from all sorts of different angles. Then a computer puts all the pictures together. This results in a very detailed picture of the inside of the body. The CT scan can show exactly where a tumor is, how big it is, and how close it is to other organs. Because CT scans can be taken from many different angles, they give doctors a better picture of organs and soft tissues than regular X-rays do.[4]

Ultrasound scans use painless sound waves to build a picture of what is inside the body. The machine has a hand-held transducer that sends sound waves. As the transducer is passed over the body, sound waves bounce off organs and bones. The rebounding waves are then picked up again by the same transducer. The transducer is attached to a computer that uses the wave patterns to create pictures of the inside of the body.[5]

A PET, or positron emission tomography, scan is a nuclear medicine imaging test. In these scans, a radioactive element called an isotope, or a tracer, is injected into the patient's body. The radiologist uses a special camera that can detect the radioactivity. Unlike the other imaging tests (which show the body's anatomy) nuclear imaging shows how certain substances move through the body. The tracer used depends on what type of tissue is being scanned. For example, one isotope that can be used in a PET scan is a radioactive sugar called fluorodeoxyglucose, or FDG. Different cells in the body take up more or less of the sugar depending on how fast they are growing. Because cancer cells are growing rapidly, they are more likely to take up large amounts of sugar, creating what is called a "hot spot" that shows up on the scan.[6] The small amount of radioactivity that the isotope gives off is not enough to do any damage. It does not harm the patient or others nearby because it decays quickly, usually in a few hours or days.[7]

Blood Tests

Along with imaging tests, blood tests can also be used to look for evidence of cancer. In one type of routine blood test, called a complete blood count, or CBC, the number of red blood cells, white blood cells, and platelets are counted. This test is also known as full blood count (FBC), a full blood exam (FBE), or a blood panel. CBCs can help doctors detect and monitor blood cancers like leukemia, lymphoma, and myeloma. Leukemia causes abnormalities in the number of white blood cells. Different types of leukemia affect the white blood cell count differently; some result in very high white blood cell counts while other types lower the number of white blood cells. Lymphoma and myeloma both interfere with the production of red blood cells. Doctors do not use blood cell counts alone to determine whether a patient has a blood cancer or not, but an abnormal CBC can signal that more testing is needed.

Blood chemistry tests may also be preformed on a sample of blood. Chemicals in the blood, called markers or biomarkers, can sometimes indicate that cancer is present. A number of different biomarkers are used to help determine if a person has cancer of the ovaries, pancreas, or testicles. At this time it is not clear how useful these markers are.

A blood sample may also be used to study a patient's chromosomes directly to see if he or she has chromosomal abnormalities that are specific to certain cancers. These blood tests are called cytogenetics tests.

Histological Studies

During a biopsy, a surgeon may send some tissue to the hospital's laboratory. A pathologist there can quick-freeze some of this tissue, take a thin slice of it, stain the cells, and look at them under the microscope. By doing this while the patient is still in surgery, the pathologist can tell the surgeon if the tumor is cancerous and should be completely removed. The surgeon can also learn how much surrounding tissue needs to be taken out to make sure as many cancer cells as possible are removed.

After the biopsy, the pathologist may imbed some of the patient's tumor tissue in a block of paraffin, a manmade waxy substance. The paraffin makes the tissue hard so it is easier for the pathologist to slice it into thin sections. Once the tissue is cut up, the slices can be stained and looked at under a microscope. This is done to give the doctor a more accurate diagnosis. Depending on what types of tests the pathologist does on the tissue sample, it may take a few days or a week or more to get the results of these lab tests.

Another procedure that can be done on biopsied tissue is called immunohistochemistry. In this procedure, monoclonal antibodies, chemicals that are attracted to certain proteins on a cell's surface, are labeled with a fluorescent dye. All cell surfaces contain a variety of proteins. Some of those proteins are found only on a particular type of cell. For example, if a fluorescent tag attracted to a protein only on lymph cells is found in the stomach, the pathologist can tell that the cell began in the lymphatic system and not the stomach.

Prognosis

The first thing most people want to know when they are diagnosed with cancer is how long they will live. The answer is called the patient's prognosis. The prognosis is an estimate of the person's chances of surviving a certain amount of time after treatment. This number is based on what has happened to a

This shows a PET (positive emission tomography) scan of the brain. The red area indicates a highly malignant brain tumor.

large group of patients diagnosed with the same type of cancer. Because the prognosis is an average, some patients will do better than the average and some will do worse. Whether a patient will do worse or better depends on several factors.

One factor is age. People are diagnosed with cancer at different ages. A twenty-year-old whose cancer is in remission will probably live longer than a seventy-year-old in remission. Also, some people tolerate cancer treatment better than others. Older people, for example, tend to have other health factors that might make them too weak or ill to continue with treatment. Another factor in prognosis estimates is that different people react differently to the same treatment. So, it is almost impossible to say exactly what an individual outcome will be. But treatments get better over time and new treatments are found every year. Advances in the fight against cancer may not be reflected in today's prognosis figures.

Treating Cancer

After diagnosis and staging studies have been completed, cancer treatment can start. Treating cancer is difficult. Cancer is not just one disease, but many. Two different types of cancer may have some of the same characteristics, but they may also have some very different ones. Also, cancer cells are abnormal. As they grow, they can change, or mutate. When the cells mutate, treatments that were previously working may not work anymore and doctors must come up with alternate treatment plans. Therefore, each cancer must be treated differently.

Doctors base treatment plans on several different factors:

how the cancer may behave if it is not treated at all;

- whether it will spread;

- if it will spread, which organs it most likely will go to; and

- how soon symptoms might appear.

Some of the answers to these questions depend on the type of cancer. So doctors need to know exactly what type of cancer and what stage the cancer is in so that they can make informed treatment recommendations.

Sometimes doctors recommend no treatment at all. That is because some cancers grow so slowly, they do not need immediate treatment. Patients with these types of cancers, however, do need to be watched closely by a doctor.[1]

Surgery

Surgery is the oldest form of treatment for cancer. For many cancers that have not spread throughout the body, surgery still offers the best chance of a cure even today. Surgery may be used for one or several of the following reasons: to diagnose and/or stage cancer; as a curative or debulking measure; as a preventive measure; or as a palliative, supportive, or restorative measure.

Biopsy: A biopsy is surgery to diagnose cancer. Biopsies are used to determine if someone has cancer, what type of cancer they have, and if, and how far, the cancer has spread.

Curative surgery: Depending on the type of cancer and what stage it is in, surgery can completely remove the mass of cancer cells. This is called curative surgery, which may be followed up with chemotherapy and/or radiation to make sure all of the cancer cells have been killed. Even if not all of the cancer cells can be cut out, because to do so might damage some nearby organ, a surgeon might try to debulk the tumor. Debulking a tumor means to make it smaller. Making the tumor smaller may make future treatments like chemotherapy or radiation more effective because there are not as many cancer cells that need to be killed.

However, the added risk from surgery may not be worthwhile if not enough of the tumor can be removed. Doctors do not usually use surgery just to debulk a tumor.

Preventive surgery: Preventive surgery can be used to remove masses or growths, such as polyps in the colon, which have not yet turned cancerous. This type of surgery might also be used if a person has a genetic condition that increases the risk of developing cancer. For example, women who inherit either of the BRCA1 or BRCA2 genes are three to seven times more likely to develop breast cancer than women without mutations in either of these genes. Because of this higher risk, some women with the BRCA1 or BRCA2 gene decide to have their breasts removed (double mastectomy) as a preventive measure, before the breast cancer has a chance to form.

Palliative surgery: Palliative surgery is used to treat the symptoms of advanced cancers. This type of surgery is not designed to cure the cancer, but to treat pain or disability that is caused by advanced cancer. The main focus of palliative surgery is to improve the patient's quality of life. For example, if a mass is pressing on nerves and causing pain, doctors may be able to debulk the tumor and relieve the pressure.[2]

Supportive surgery: Supportive surgery helps enable other treatments. For example, many cancer patients have surgery to install a port, a small, round plastic or metal disc that is inserted under the patient's skin. A catheter, a small thin tube, connects the port to a large vein, usually in the chest. The port allows doctors and nurses to easily take blood and to give chemotherapy drugs to the patient without using a needle for each treatment.

Restorative surgery: Restorative surgery is the same as reconstructive, or plastic, surgery. This type of surgery is used to restore someone's appearance. Restorative surgery is commonly used after removing a facial cancer or a breast.[3]

Chemotherapy

Chemotherapy is a treatment that uses drugs to try to kill cancer cells. Because the drugs travel through the bloodstream, chemotherapy affects the whole body instead of just the cancer site. Most chemotherapy treatments involve three or four different drugs that try to kill the cancer cells in different ways. The different drugs are given to the patient on a specific schedule. The schedule is called a **protocol**.[4]

The drugs in a chemotherapy protocol kill cancer cells by targeting different processes going on in the cancer cells. For example, one drug might make it impossible for the cancer cell to copy its DNA so it cannot divide. Another drug might prevent cell division by not allowing formation of certain enzymes the cell needs to copy itself. Or a drug may stop the formation of physical structures that the cell needs to divide correctly. By using different drugs, doctors hope that at least one of them will be effective in killing the cancer cells. Doctors also hope that if the cancer cells mutate, one of the drugs will still work. Because each of the drugs works to kill the cancer cells in different ways, the cancer does not become resistant to therapy. A cancer cell may mutate so that one of the drugs will not work, but it is unlikely that it would mutate to the point that none of the drugs would work.[5]

For many cancers that have not spread throughout the body, surgery offers the best chance of a cure.

Almost all chemotherapy drugs have some side effects. The drugs are designed to kill fast-growing cancer cells. But because they are powerful drugs and they travel through the bloodstream, they kill some normal cells, too. Normal cells that divide quickly, like those in the mouth, digestive tract, bone marrow, and hair follicles, are most often affected. Because the drugs attack these cells, side effects can include fatigue, hair loss, loss of appetite, weight loss, nausea, and vomiting. Not all

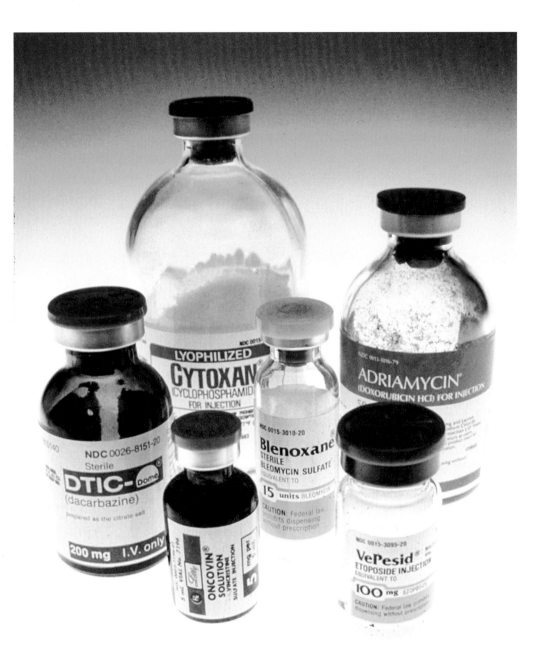

Chemotherapy refers to the use of drugs to kill cancer cells. Shown are a variety of chemotherapy drugs.

chemotherapy drugs make patients sick, and not all cause the patient's hair to fall out. It depends on the drug and the patient's tolerance for it. However, the side effects are usually temporary and go away when the chemotherapy is finished.

Drugs called protectors may also be added to the chemotherapy protocol. Protectors are drugs that lessen the side effects of the treatment. Modifiers or sensitizers may be added to the protocol, too. These drugs do not kill cancer cells directly, but they boost the effectiveness of other chemotherapy drugs in the protocol.

Radiation

Radiation therapy can be used alone or together with surgery or chemotherapy. Radiation therapy does not go throughout the body like chemotherapy does; it is targeted to just the area where the cancer is found.

A machine called a linear accelerator delivers one type of radiation therapy. The linear accelerator produces powerful X rays that are about one thousand times stronger than the regular X-ray machines used for diagnosis. These machines produce enough energy to kill cells, both tumor cells and normal cells.

Radiation works by damaging the cancer cell's DNA and making it impossible for the cells to grow and divide. Because this type of radiation therapy comes from a machine outside of the patient's body, it is called external radiation therapy. External radiation therapy does not make patients radioactive. They are not a threat to the people around them.[6]

Internal radiation therapy, or brachytherapy, involves placing a source of radiation, in a small capsule or implant, inside the patient's body at the site of the cancer. The radioactive source depends on the type of cancer. Sources include radioactive iodine, strontium, phosphorous, palladium, cesium, iridium, phosphate, or cobalt. Radioactive iodine, for example, is used to treat thyroid cancer. And radioactive strontium can be used to treat cancers that have spread to the bones. Scientists are working to identify other sources that might work, too.

Sometimes the implant is temporary; the radiation source usually only lasts between two to four days before it breaks down into something that is not radioactive. Visitors may be limited during those few days so that they are not exposed to radiation. In other cases, a permanent implant may be used. The radioactive material in a permanent implant also decays, or breaks down, until there is no more radioactive material left. But permanent implants often contain much lower amounts of radiation than temporary implants so there is usually no danger to people around the patient and no restrictions on visits from family and friends.[7]

Bone Marrow Transplants

Chemotherapy and radiation treatments are designed to attack the quickly growing and dividing cancer cells. But sometimes they attack normal cells which also divide quickly, such as bone marrow cells. Without healthy bone marrow, a person may not be able to make enough blood cells. Red blood cells carry oxygen to other cells in the body. White blood cells are important in preventing infection. And platelets help the blood to clot when a person is injured. All of these blood cells are made by the bone marrow and can be affected by chemotherapy or radiation. If too many of the cells in the bone marrow are destroyed, the person may need to undergo a procedure called a bone marrow transplant (BMT).

Bone marrow transplants can be done using the patient's own bone marrow cells or by using someone else's. If the patient's own bone marrow cells are going to be used, these cells are taken from the patient before chemotherapy or radiation treatment begins. This is called an **autologous transplant**. If someone else's bone marrow cells are used, the BMT is called an **allogeneic transplant**. The donor in an allogeneic transplant is

Radiation has been used as a cancer treatment for decades. This 1957 photograph shows the first patient treated with radiation for retinoblastoma, a tumor on the retina of the eye. He survived and retained the sight in one eye.

usually a close relative of the patient, such as a parent or a sibling. The donor's bone marrow tissue type must match the patient's tissue type as closely as possible. If the tissue types do not match closely, the patient may develop **graft-versus-host disease**, in which the donor's immune cells, present in the bone marrow that was transplanted into the patient, attack the patient's tissues.[8] Doctors usually prescribe drugs that suppress the patient's immune system to prevent graft-versus-host disease.

BMT is also used to treat certain types of cancers, most commonly lymphomas and leukemias. Leukemia is a cancer of the bone marrow and lymphoma is a cancer that starts in lymph cells, part of the immune system. Other cancers treated using BMT include neuroblastoma, a cancer that affects immature nerve cells, and multiple myeloma, a cancer that begins in the white blood cells, which make antibodies to fight infections.[9] Scientists are studying other cancers to determine whether BMT might be an effective way of fighting them too.

Immunotherapy

Immunotherapy, sometimes called biological therapy, uses the body's immune system to fight cancer or to lessen side effects of certain treatments. For example, some biological therapies stimulate the patient's bone marrow to make more red blood cells, white blood cells, and platelets. If the chemotherapy is killing off some of the patient's healthy bone marrow cells, this type of immunotherapy can help the patient's bone marrow to recover and make the needed cells.

Scientists are also studying how to make certain antibodies, called monoclonal antibodies, in the laboratory that might be able to help find certain types of cancers. These antibodies circulate through the body's bloodstream. They can detect certain proteins on the outside of cancer cells. When an antibody finds the protein it is looking for, it attaches to the cancer cell. This marks the cancer cell for destruction by other cells in the patient's immune system. Two types of monoclonal antibodies have already been approved for cancer treatment by the FDA. One type is used to treat breast cancer and the other to treat non-Hodgkin's lymphoma.[10]

Clinical Trials

Clinical trials, which are sometimes called research studies, test new drugs or treatments designed to help people with cancer. These drugs, called investigational drugs, have not been approved by the FDA yet. They are still experimental. Before a drug is allowed to be used on humans, it must go through several steps.

The first step in the process of drug development is testing the drug in the laboratory. Laboratory tests usually include testing the drug on cancer cells in a petri dish, for example, and in a laboratory animal. If the results of these laboratory tests seem promising, the drug may move into phase I clinical trials.

Phase I. During a phase I clinical trial, the drug will be used in humans for the first time. Phase I trials usually involve a small number of people. This part of the process determines if the drug is safe, how much of the drug should be taken, and what kind of side effects it might have. If the drug appears to be safe, with minimal side effects, it may go on to phase II clinical trials.[11]

Phase II. During a phase II clinical trial, the drug is given to a slightly larger number of people. The idea is to make sure the drug is safe in many different types of people and to see how effective the drug is at treating the condition that it is meant to treat. If the drug passes this phase, it goes on to phase III.

Phase III. In a phase III clinical trial, hundreds or, sometimes, thousands of people are given the drug.[12] If the drug passes this phase, it can be submitted for FDA approval, the last step in the process. Once a drug has FDA approval, it can be marketed and sold in the United States.

Patients interested in being involved in a clinical trial will need to decide, with their doctor's help, if they can take an experimental drug. Doctors can help patients find out whether they are eligible for the clinical trial, and if it is worth it for them to take a drug that may or may not help.

Effectiveness of Treatment

Doctors usually check how a patient is responding to treatment during the course of therapy and at the end of treatment. Many of the same tests used to diagnose cancer are used to determine how effective the treatment has been. Doctors use several terms in describing the cancer's response to treatment.[13]

Complete response is also sometimes called complete remission. This means that the tumor has completely disappeared. This does not mean that the cancer will never come back, but at the moment, no cancer can be detected. If the cancer does recur after complete remission has been achieved, it is called a relapse. Partial response, or partial remission, means that the tumor is still there, but that it has shrunk to less than half of its original size. Minor response, or minor remission, means that the tumor is responding to treatment and shrinking somewhat, but that it is still more than half of its original size. When doctors say that a patient has stable disease, this means that the tumor did not shrink during treatment, but that it did not get any bigger either. Progressive disease, however, means that the tumor did not respond to treatment and that it grew at least 25 percent larger than it was before treatment began. In general, patients who do not experience complete remission will need some kind of further treatment.

Dealing With Cancer

While cancer diagnosis and treatment are necessary, they can be quite unpleasant or worse. But learning to live with cancer and cope with the side effects of treatment is becoming more important, because, as treatments get better, more people are surviving this disease.

When someone is first diagnosed with cancer, it can be overwhelming. But the first thing to remember is that there are very few cancers that need to be treated as an emergency. So there is time for patients to gather information, talk to their doctors, get second opinions, and speak to other people who have been in the same situation. Gathering this type of information can help newly diagnosed patients make informed decisions about their medical treatment and help them to prepare.

Where can patients get their information? Doctors and nurses are some of the most reliable sources of information. Books and magazine or newspaper articles might help, too. The Internet is also full of information about cancer, but not every Web site can be trusted. A lot of the information on the Internet has not been checked by experts. When looking for reliable information about cancer, it is best to stick with respected Web sites such as those of the American Cancer Society or the National Institutes of Health, which are among the Internet addresses in the back of this book.

Dealing With Feelings

When people first receive the diagnosis of cancer, they are likely to feel anxious and frightened. They will need to gather all the information they can, but it is possible that they will feel overwhelmed. They may have difficulty concentrating on much of anything, much less complicated medical information. Some people have preconceived ideas about what a cancer diagnosis means, too. These ideas might come from family or friends who have had cancer, from news stories, or from information from the Internet. Remember, though, there are many different types of cancer and many different types of people, and each person's circumstances are unique.

Many times, just understanding what cancer is, where it comes from, and what doctors know about treating a specific type of cancer can soothe fears. Accurate information may help them feel a little more in control and allow them to fully participate in their medical care.

Shock, disbelief, fear, anxiety, guilt, sadness, grief, depression, and anger are some of the more common emotions people experience upon hearing the news that they or someone they love has cancer. Not everyone feels all of these emotions, but for people who do, all of these are very normal responses. Not everyone deals with emotions the same way, either. Talking to someone about these feelings can sometimes help.

If you know someone who has been diagnosed with cancer, you can provide support by simply listening. Try to be the best friend you can be. There is no perfect way to act or thing to say. Just try to be yourself and treat the other person the same way you always have.

Sometimes, people may not want to talk about their feelings, treatments, or general health. If this is the case, try to respect that decision. They just might need a break from thinking about cancer and everything that goes along with it. They may want to do something with friends that they did before they got sick. But also try to let it be known that whenever they are ready to talk, you will be there to listen.

Support Groups

A support group is a group of people who are all going through the same type of situation. Talking to a cancer support group helps some people work through the emotions of a cancer diagnosis. The group can also help support the cancer patient through the rigors of cancer treatment. Knowing that other people have gone through the same things and have dealt with the same emotions can sometimes help.

Support groups are not just for people who have cancer, either. If you have a parent or sibling who has been diagnosed with cancer, there are support groups for friends and relatives, too. You might be surprised to find that other people are dealing with the same issues you are and that talking to them can help make you feel better.

Alternative Medicine

Sometimes people turn to cancer therapies that have not yet been proven scientifically. These are called alternative,

FIGHT CANCER WITH KNOWLEDGE

ENLIST IN THE WOMEN'S FIELD ARMY
AMERICAN SOCIETY FOR THE CONTROL OF CANCER

An old poster from the American Society for the Control of Cancer echoes Mary Lumapas's motto: Knowledge is power.

Some people with cancer worry that they will lose their hair. Hair loss is often a side effect of cancer treatment. But it is almost always temporary; the hair will grow back. (One exception is loss caused by radiation for brain tumors, which is often permanent.)

In the meantime, some people look at this as an opportunity to try a new look—wearing hats, wigs, scarves, or even just going bald.

complementary, or unconventional treatments. They can also be unproven, unorthodox, or even unsound or questionable, depending on the type of therapy. Relaxation therapies, such as aromatherapy, meditation, or yoga, herbal medicines, vitamin treatments, special diets, bioelectromagnetics, and massage are some examples of alternative therapies. Some of these treatments are starting to get more attention from medical doctors. And some doctors may advise their patients to use an alternative therapy in addition to their more conventional treatments. They might recommend relaxation, massage, or meditation, for example, to help patients with their overall feeling of well-being. Or they may advise a specific change in diet to counteract the side effects from chemotherapy or radiation therapy.

It is always best for the patient to ask the doctor's opinion of unconventional treatment. Some therapies, especially those that involve diet, herbal medications, or extra vitamins could inter-act negatively with the patient's other treatments. The patient could get sicker or other treatments could be less effective.[1]

Taking Care of Yourself and Others

If you are dealing with a parent or a sibling with cancer, do not forget to take care of yourself, too. Staying connected with your friends by going to school, participating in or attending school sporting events, or going to a friend's house once in a while can help relieve some of the stress. Take the time to relax and make sure you are getting enough sleep. Eat a healthy diet and get plenty of exercise. Exercise will also probably help you sleep better.

If you feel like you need to do something, it might make you feel better to get involved by helping others raise money for cancer research. For example, you could join a walk like the American Cancer Society's overnight Relay for Life. You could hold a bake sale and donate the money to an organization that supports cancer research.

You can also help someone going through treatment by spending time together. Try to have some fun. Humor seems to make everyone feel better. Try to be upbeat, but still "real." In other words, do not deny that the person is sick, but try not to dwell on it either. Offer to keep a joint journal. Write songs, poems, or stories together. People appreciate it when someone takes the time to try to make them feel better.

In Mary Lumapas's opinion, the best thing a person can do for someone who has been diagnosed with cancer is to treat them normally. "I'm just normal. Like anyone else," she said.[2] When Mary was going through treatment, it hurt her feelings when classmates stopped asking her to come to birthday parties and sleepovers. Maybe they thought she would be too ill to come. "Sure,

If you know someone who has been diagnosed with cancer, you can provide support by simply listening. Try to be the best friend you can be.

sometimes I was too sick to go, but it is still nice to be asked and to make my own decisions," Mary said.[3]

Some people are worried that cancer is contagious, but it is not. Others are afraid that they will say or do the wrong thing and upset the person. "Don't worry about that," said Mary. "Just treat the person the same way you did before." Invite your friend to all the fun things you would have before you found out about the cancer. For Mary, her brother Rio has been a big help. He helps to keep her connected to regular things, like what is going on at school.

In summer, Mary goes to Reaching Out to Cancer Kids (R.O.C.K.) camp. R.O.C.K. is one of the American Cancer Society's programs in Florida. When it opened in 1976, it was the first camp for children with cancer in the United States. R.O.C.K. camp is free and open to any seven- to sixteen-year-old who lives in Florida and is being treated for any type of

Exercise can be a big stress reliever for the family and friends of someone with cancer.

cancer. Like every other summer camp, it has activities like swimming, horseback riding, and arts and crafts.[4] R.O.C.K. is not the only camp run by the American Cancer Society. Among the other camps across the United States are Camp Kemo (in South Carolina), Camp UKANDU (in Oregon), and Camp Can-Do (in Pennsylvania).

Mary's parents, Gaythee and Fabian Lumapas, work very hard to help Mary lead as normal a life as possible. "I don't want Mary's every childhood memory to be about hospitals, doctors, and chemotherapy," said Gaythee.[5] The family helps Mary deal with her illness with love and humor.

There is no way to know if Mary Lumapas's cancer might come back again. She may grow up strong and healthy and able to pursue her dream of becoming a pediatric oncologist, a doctor who specializes in childhood cancers. With her experience, intelligence, and zest for life, she could help a lot of kids who find themselves in her situation. To Mary, attitude is everything. "You can't go around saying—Woe is me," she said. "I mean, what's the point? Everybody's going to die someday. Just get on with life."[6] And that is exactly what Mary is doing.

The Fight Against Cancer

During the last fifty years, cancer diagnosis and treatment have come a long way. But there is still no cure for cancer. Scientists continue to look for ways to kill cancer cells without harming normal ones. There are several promising avenues.

Monoclonal antibodies are already being used to help doctors diagnose cancer. Now researchers are using them to treat the disease by having them attach to tumor cells, marking them for destruction by the body's immune system. Scientists are also researching ways to have monoclonal antibodies deliver chemotherapy or a radioactive drug directly to the surface of a cancer cell, in order to kill it. The antibodies may also block specific receptors on a cancer cell's membrane, interfering with the chemicals that cancer cells need to grow. If the receptor on a cancer cell's membrane was blocked, it could also prevent the cell from getting rid of certain chemicals that would eventually poison the cell. Several monoclonal antibodies have already been approved to treat cancer, and scientists are looking for more.[1]

Another approach scientists are taking is the development of targeted drugs to prevent cancer cells from growing and dividing. One of these drugs, imatinib or Gleevec, has become the standard of care for people with chronic myelogenous leukemia (CML). Scientists are still studying imatinib because it may help treat other cancers as well.[2]

Scientists are also looking into ways to use gene therapy to replace faulty tumor suppressors or oncogenes. They may also be able to insert genes into tumor cells that would make them more vulnerable to chemotherapy drugs or radiation. Or they could insert genes into normal cells that would make them less susceptible to harm from radiation or chemotherapy drugs. This would allow doctors to use higher doses of these traditional treatments. The main problem scientists have with this technique is the lack of a suitable carrier to get the corrected genes into the genome.[3]

Targeted Drugs

From 1999 to 2004, eleven drugs specifically designed to target cancer cells were developed and approved by the FDA. These drugs work by either blocking the growth of cancer cells or preventing them from spreading. They do this by interfering with the normal activities of certain chemicals inside the cancer cells. Because scientists call these chemicals "molecular targets," these drugs are often called molecularly targeted drugs or therapies.

Gleevec is one of these drugs. In white blood cells, one particular type of enzyme is responsible for telling the cells when to grow and divide and when to stop. This enzyme is like a light switch. In patients with chronic myelogenous leukemia (CML), the enzyme is stuck in the "on" position. This causes the white blood cells to grow and divide out of control. The drug Gleevec can turn this enzyme "off" and abnormal leukemia cells stop dividing.

Herceptin, another targeted drug that is a monoclonal antibody, is used to fight breast cancer. In some breast cancer cases, cells produce too much of a protein called HER2. Herceptin can detect cells that have too many copies of this protein. When the drug finds a cell with too much HER2, it attaches itself to these abnormal cells. This attachment does two things—it prevents the protein from sending signals to continue growing and it alerts the body's immune system that the cell is a cancer cell and should be destroyed.

These drugs target specific chemicals in cancer cells, so cancer patients encounter fewer treatment-related side effects than they do with traditional chemotherapy. In addition, these drugs do not kill as many normal cells.

Epigenetics

Geneticists have found that the order of base pairs in the DNA molecule is just one piece of the puzzle when it comes to genetics. The other piece is called epigenetics. Epigenetics is the study of changes to a person's DNA that does not involve changing the order of the DNA "alphabet." This can include the addition of chemicals to the DNA molecule that can turn genes "on" and "off."

The pattern of chemical additions to the DNA is passed down from parent to child. The chemicals added to the DNA molecule are called "marks." Cells use these marks to tell which set of genes was inherited from the father and which came from the mother. The marks do not just tell which genes were inherited from which parent, though; they also tell the cell which set of genes to use to make proteins. These genes are known as imprinted genes.[4]

Scientists now think that imprinted genes play a big role in the development of cancer. The imprinting may tell the cell to turn off, or not read, some genes while switching others on. For example, scientists have found that the tumor suppressor genes on the chromosomes from the mother are usually turned on, but if the DNA molecule has had a chemical addition, these genes may be mistakenly switched off.

There is still no cure for cancer. Scientists continue to look for ways to kill cancer cells without harming normal ones.

Functional oncogenes, the ones that promote cell growth, on the other hand, seem to be passed down through the father's chromosomes. One copy of an oncogene gives a cell just the right amount of protein to allow it to grow, but not to grow out of control. Oncogenes are also present on the mother's chromosomes but are usually switched off. If the maternal chromosome loses its marks, and its imprinting is lost, the maternal gene will be transcribed and translated into protein, too. The result could lead to too much protein and uncontrolled cell growth.[5]

Changes in epigenetic marks happen the same way changes in the DNA molecule do: mistakes in copying the genome from one generation of cells to the next. But exactly how the marks are added or lost is not well understood yet.[6] Some research seems to show that environmental factors, such as diet, may cause changes in these epigenetic marks. Scientists are now trying to understand when the marks are easiest to modify due to these environmental factors.[7]

Scientists are also looking for ways to use their knowledge of epigenetic modification to help them treat and possibly prevent cancer. One way they could do this is by trying to find a way to reactivate tumor suppressor genes that have accidentally been turned off. They are looking into ways to combine dietary changes or other treatments with chemotherapy drugs, which are known to have an effect on epigenetics, trying to improve the drugs' effectiveness. Scientists are also trying to find ways that they might be able to improve how an individual's cancer

Purified DNA glows under ultraviolet light. Epigenetics—the study of changes to DNA that do not involve changing the order of the DNA "alphabet"—is a promising avenue in cancer research.

risk is predicted. They could do this by identifying changes in the DNA early. They hope that a person's cancer risk could be reduced with changes in their environment and diet.[8]

Angiogenesis Inhibitors

In order for cancer cells to grow and spread, they need oxygen and nutrients. They get these things from the blood vessels of nearby healthy tissue. This is called **angiogenesis**. Some cancer researchers are looking for chemicals, called angiogenesis inhibitors, which would block cancer cells from forming new blood vessels. Without the blood vessels, the cells would die.[9] Scientists are also working on several drugs that would destroy existing blood vessels in cancerous tumors and prevent the tumor from forming new ones. One such drug, called bevacizumab or Avastin, has already been approved by the FDA for this use.[10]

Who knows what scientists will come up with in the future? There have already been many discoveries that prolong lives as well as make cancer treatment less toxic. "Our ultimate goal is . . . [to] find the right treatment for the right patient and cure the disease. Unfortunately, we're not there yet," Dr. Francisco J. Esteva, a breast cancer specialist at the M.D. Anderson Cancer Center in Houston, told *The New York Times* in June 2008.[11] It is possible, however, that one day scientists will find the secret and cancer will be a disease of the past.

Chapter Notes

Introduction

1. Personal interview with Gaythee Lumapas, July 24, 2007.

2. Ibid.

3. Personal interview with Mary Lumapas, July 24, 2007.

4. Ibid.

5. Ibid.; personal interview with Gaythee Lumapas, July 24, 2007.

Chapter 1: What Is Cancer?

1. "How Many Different Types of Cancer Are There?" *Cancer Research UK*, December 13, 2006, <http://www.cancerhelp.org.uk/help/default.asp?page=2545> (February 5, 2008).

2. Leon Browder and Laurie Iten, eds., "Programmed Cell Death in Development," *Dynamic Development*, March 3, 1998, <http://www.acs.ucalgary.ca/~browder/apoptosis.html> (February 5, 2007).

3. C. Norman Coleman, *Understanding Cancer*, 2nd edition (Baltimore: The Johns Hopkins University Press, 1998), p. 31.

4. Robert A. Weinberg, *One Renegade Cell: How Cancer Begins* (New York: Basic Books, 1998), p. 2.

5. Robert Buckman, *What You Really Need to Know About Cancer* (Baltimore: The Johns Hopkins University Press, 1997), pp. 13–14.

6. Ibid.

7. American Society for Microbiology, "DNA: the Blueprint for Life," *Microbe World*, n.d., <http://www.microbeworld.org/know/dna.aspx> (February 5, 2008).

8. "Who Gets Cancer?" *American Cancer Society*, 2008, <http://www.cancer.org/docroot/CRI/content/CRI_2_4_1x_Who_gets_cancer.asp?rnav=cri> (February 5, 2008).

9. Carolyn D. Runowicz, Sheldon H. Cherry, and Dianne Partie Lange, *The Answer to Cancer* (Emmaus, Pa.: Rodale, 2004), p. 9.

10. "Known and Probable Carcinogens," *American Cancer Society*, February 3, 2006, <http://www.cancer.org/docroot/PED/content/PED_1_3x_Known_and_Probable_Carcinogens.asp?sitearea=PED> (February 12, 2008).

11. Coleman, pp. 34–35; "Genetic Testing for Breast and Ovarian Cancer Risk: It's Your Choice," *National Cancer Institute*, n.d., <http://www.nci.nih.gov/cancertopics/Genetic-Testing-for-Breast-and-Ovarian-Cancer-Risk> (February 12, 2008).

Chapter 2: Cancer Through History

1. "The Harold Varmus Papers," *Profiles in Science*, National Library of Medicine, n.d., <http://profiles.nlm.nih.gov/MV/Views/Exhibit/narrative/oncogenes.html> (August 29, 2007).

2. "Cancer: a Historic Perspective." *SEER's Web-Based Training Modules*, U.S. National Cancer Institute's Surveillance, Epidemiology and End Results (SEER) Program, n.d., <http://training.seer.cancer.gov/module_cancer_disease/unit1_historic_perspective.html> (August 29, 2007).

3. Robert H. Wilkins, "Edwin Smith Surgical Papyrus," *Cyber Museum of Neurosurgery*, July 2006, <http://www.neurosurgery.org/cybermuseum/pre20th/epapyrus.html> (August 29, 2007).

4. "History of Cancer." *Medicine World*, n.d., <http://medicineworld.org/cancer/history.html> (August 29, 2007).

5. "The History of Cancer," *American Cancer Society*, March 25, 2002, <http://www.cancer.org/docroot/CRI/content/CRI_2_6x_the_history_of_cancer_72.asp?sitearea=CRI> (August 29, 2007).

6. "Cancer: a Historic Perspective."

7. "History of Cancer," *Medicine World.*

8. Ibid.

9. "Cancer: a Historic Perspective."

10. "History of Cancer," *Medicine World.*

11. "The History of Cancer," *American Cancer Society.*

12. "Cancer: a Historic Perspective."

13. "The 18th Century. Clinical Anatomy and the Pathology of Organs," *History of Medicine*, September 2004, <http://pacs.unica.it/biblio/lesson6.htm> (August 29, 2007).

14. Sharon Lane, "Cancer History," *Rare Cancer Alliance*, June 2005, <http://www.rare-cancer.org/history-of-cancer.html> (August 29, 2007).

15. "Timeline of Cancer," *Cancer Quest: History of Cancer*, December 2006, <http://www.cancerquest.org/index.cfm?page=2405> (August 29, 2007).

16. "The History of Cancer," *American Cancer Society.*

17. "History of Cancer," *Medicine World.*

18. Barbara Marte, "Milestone 2: Cancer as a Genetic Disease," *Nature Milestones: Cancer*, April 2006, <http://www.nature.com/milestones/milecancer/full/milecancer02.html> (August 29, 2007).

19. Ibid.

20. Ibid.

21. Lane.

22. "Timeline of Cancer."

23. Lane.

24. "What is Chemotherapy?" *American Cancer Society,* November 2006, <http://www.cancer.org/docroot/ETO/ content/ETO_1_4X_What_Is_Chemotherapy.asp?sitearea= ETO> (August 29, 2007).

25. "The History of Cancer," *American Cancer Society.*

26. C. Norman Coleman, *Understanding Cancer,* 2nd edition (Baltimore: The Johns Hopkins University Press, 2006), p. 44.

27. "Definition of Squamous Cell Carcinoma," *National Cancer Institute,* n.d., <http://www.cancer.gov/Templates db_alpha.aspx?CdrID=46595> (August 29, 2007).

Chapter 3: Risky Business

1. "Cancer Risk Factors," *SEER's Web-Based Training Modules,* U.S. National Cancer Institute's Surveillance, Epidemiology and End Results (SEER) Program, n.d., <http://training. seer.cancer.gov/module_cancer_disease/unit2_whatscancer4_ risk_factors.html> (August 28, 2007).

2. Ibid.

3. "What are the Risk Factors for Cancer?" *American Cancer Society,* 2008, <http://www.cancer.org/docroot/CRI/content/ CRI_2_4_2x_What_are_the_risk_factors_for_cancer_72.asp> (August 28, 2007).

4. "Cancer Risk Factors."

5. "Known and Probable Carcinogens," *American Cancer Society,* n.d., <http://www.cancer.org/docroot/PED/content/PED_1_ 3x_Known_and_Probable_Carcinogens.asp?sitearea=PED> (August 29, 2007).

6. "Your Environment and Cancer," *Cancer Help UK,* June 2007, <http://www.cancerhelp.org.uk/help/ default.asp?page=121> (August 27, 2007).

7. "Smokeless Tobacco and Cancer," *National Cancer Institute* Fact Sheet, May 2003, <http://www.smokefree.gov/Docs2/ SmokelessTobacco_Q&A.pdf> (August 20, 2007).

8. "Secondhand Smoke Fact Sheet," *American Lung Association*, June 2007, <http://www.lungusa.org/site/pp.asp?c= dvLUK9O0E&b=35422> (August 29, 2007).

9. "Cancer Risk Factors."

10. Ibid.

11. "Diet Causing Cancer," *Cancer Help UK*, June 2007, <http://www.cancerhelp.org.uk/help/default.asp?page=120> (August 29, 2007).

12. "U.S. Report Adds to List of Carcinogens," *New York Times*, May 16, 2000, <http://query.nytimes.com/gst/fullpage. html?sec=health&res=9801E4D6103BF935A25756C0A9669 C8B63&n=Top%2fNews%2fHealth%2fDiseases%2c%20Co nditions%2c%20and%20Health%20Topics%2fCancer> (August 29, 2007).

13. "Diet Causing Cancer."

14. "Where There's Smoke ... " *MIT Medical*, 2006, <http:// web.mit.edu/medical/mithealth/summer2006/stories/story2_1 .shtml> (August 29, 2007).

15. "Diet Causing Cancer."

16. Larry Thompson, "Sunscreen, Skin Cancer, and UVA," *Health Link*, July 2000, <http://healthlink.mcw.edu/article/ 964647970.html> (August 29, 2007).

17. "Childhood Sunburn Melanoma Risk," *BBC News*, September 20, 2001, <http://news.bbc.co.uk/1/hi/health/ 1554086.stm> (August 29, 2007).

18. Thompson.

19. Ibid.

20. "Radon," *U. S. Environmental Protection Agency*, October

2006, <http://www.epa.gov/radiation/radionuclides/radon.htm> (August 29, 2007).

21. "Radiation, Microwaves and Cancer," *Cancer Help UK*, July 2007, <http://www.cancerhelp.org.uk/help/default.asp?page=8774#non> (August 29, 2007).

22. "Your Environment and Cancer," *Cancer Help UK*, June 2007, <http://www.cancerhelp.org.uk/help/default.asp?page=121> (August 29, 2007).

23. "Cancer Risk Factors."

24. "What Causes Cancer?" *Cancer Help UK*, June 2007, <http://www.cancerhelp.org.uk/help/default.asp?page=119> (August 29, 2007).

25. "Down Syndrome-Cancer Link Studied," *Associated Press*, January 14, 2000, <http://www.downsyn.com/cancer.html> (August 29, 2007).

26. Simon Cotterill, "Fanconi Anaemia," *Children's Cancer Web*, May 2003, <http://www.cancerindex.org/ccw/fanconi.htm> (August 29, 2007).

27. "Your Environment and Cancer."

28. "Benzene," *American Cancer Society*, February 2006, <http://www.cancer.org/docroot/PED/content/PED_1_3X_Benzene.asp?sitearea=PED> (August 29, 2007).

29. "Cancer Risk Factors."

30. "Viruses and Cancer," *Cell Biology and Cancer*, n.d., <http://www.learner.org/channel/courses/biology/textbook/cancer/cancer_7.html> (August 29, 2007).

31. "Infectious Agents and Cancer," *American Cancer Society*, October 2006, <http://www.cancer.org/docroot/PED/content/PED_1_3X_Infectious_Agents_and_Cancer.asp?sitearea=PED> (August 29, 2007).

32. "What Causes Cancer?"

Chapter 4: Preventive Measures

1. "ABCD's of Melanoma," *American Melanoma Foundation,* 2006, <http://www.melanomafoundation.org/prevention/abcd.htm> (August 29, 2007).

2. "Diet Causing Cancer," *Cancer Help UK,* June 2007, <http://www.cancerhelp.org.uk/help/default.asp?page=120> (August 29, 2007).

3. "Phytochemicals," *American Cancer Society,* June 2007, <http://www.cancer.org/docroot/ETO/content/ETO_5_3x_Phytochemicals.asp> (August 29, 2007).

4. Cynthia Stein, "Can Cancer Be Prevented?" *Education Update,* April 2003, <http://www.educationupdate.com/archives/2003/apr03/issue/med-can-cancer.html> (August 29, 2007).

5. "Cancer Vaccine Fact Sheet," *National Cancer Institute,* June 2006, <http://www.cancer.gov/cancertopics/factsheet/cancervaccine> (August 29, 2007).

6. Ibid.

Chapter 5: Diagnosis

1. "Why Staging?" *SEER's Web-Based Training Modules,* U.S. National Cancer Institute's Surveillance, Epidemiology and End Results (SEER) Program, n.d., <http://training.seer.cancer.gov/module_ss2k/intro_why_staging.html> (August 29, 2007).

2. "Imaging (Radiology) Tests," *American Cancer Society,* December 2005, <http://www.cancer.org/docroot/PED/content/PED_2_3X_Imaging_Radiology_Tests.asp> (August 29, 2007).

3. "MRI Scan," *Cancer Help UK,* June 2007, <http://www.cancerhelp.org.uk/help/default.asp?page=149> (August 29, 2007).

4. "Imaging (Radiology) Tests."

5. "Ultrasound Scan," *Cancer Help UK*, June 2007, <http://www.cancerhelp.org.uk/help/default.asp?page=149> (August 29, 2007).

6. "Imaging (Radiology) Tests."

7. C. Norman Coleman, *Understanding Cancer*, 2nd edition (Baltimore: The Johns Hopkins University Press, 2006), p. 52.

8. "Fantastic Voyage with Capsule Endoscopy," *California Pacific Medical Center*, September 2001, <http://www.cpmc.org/about/press/news2001/capendoscopy.html> (August 29, 2007).

Chapter 6: Treating Cancer

1. C. Norman Coleman, *Understanding Cancer*, 2nd edition (Baltimore: The Johns Hopkins University Press, 2006), p. 15.

2. "Surgery," *American Cancer Society*, March 2007, <http://www.cancer.org/docroot/ETO/content/ETO_1_2X_Surgery.asp> (August 29, 2007).

3. Ibid.

4. Coleman, pp. 89–90.

5. Ibid.

6. Ibid., p. 100.

7. Ibid., p. 106.

8. Ibid., p. 108.

9. "Dictionary of Cancer Terms," *National Cancer Institute*, <http://www.cancer.gov/dictionary/> (August 29, 2007).

10. "Biological Therapies for Cancer: Questions and Answers," *National Cancer Institute*, June 2006, <http://www.cancer.gov/cancertopics/factsheet/Therapy/biological> (August 29, 2007).

11. "What is a Clinical Trial?" *Antigenics*, 2008, <http://www.antigenics.com/trials/about/> (August 29, 2007).

12. "The New Drug Development Process," *U. S. Food and Drug Administration*, n.d., <http://www.fda.gov/CDER/handbook/develop.htm> (August 29, 2007).

13. Coleman, pp. 60–62.

Chapter 7: Dealing With Cancer

1. C. Norman Coleman, *Understanding Cancer*, 2nd edition (Baltimore: The Johns Hopkins University Press, 2006), p. 6.

2. Personal interview with Mary Lumapas, July 24, 2007.

3. Ibid.

4. "R.O.C.K. Camp," *American Cancer Society*, 2008, <http://www.cancer.org/docroot/COM/content/div_FL/COM_5_1x_ROCK_Camp.asp> (August 27, 2007).

5. Personal interview with Gaythee Lumapas, July 24, 2007.

6. Personal interview with Mary Lumapas, July 24, 2007.

Chapter 8: The Fight Against Cancer

1. Ronald M. Bukowski and Ena Segota, "The Promise of Targeted Therapy: Cancer Drugs Become More Specific," *Cleveland Clinic Journal of Medicine*, July 2004, <http://ccjm.org/PDFFILES/Segota704.pdf> (August 30, 2007).

2. Ibid.

3. Ibid.

4. Ibid.

5. Ibid.

6. Ibid.

7. "Epigenetics: a New Frontier in Cancer Research," *AICR Science Now*, Spring 2007, <http://www.aicr.org/site/News2?JServSessionIdr011=fib2kcs952.app1a&abbr=res_&page=NewsArticle&id=11800> (August 30, 2007).

8. Ibid.

9. Mark Zimmer, *Glowing Genes: A Revolution in Biotechnology* (Amherst, N.Y.: Prometheus Books, 2005), p. 165.

10. C. Norman Coleman, *Understanding Cancer*, 2nd edition (Baltimore: The Johns Hopkins University Press, 2006), p. 39.

11. Jane Brody, "Cancer as a Disease, Not a Death Sentence," *New York Times*, June 17, 2008, <http://www.nytimes.com/2008/06/17/health/17brody.html> (June 28, 2008).

Glossary

allogeneic transplant—A transplant using a donor's bone marrow cells.

angiogenesis—The formation of new blood vessels.

autologous transplant—A transplant using the patient's own bone marrow cells that were extracted before treatment began.

benign—Tumors that are not cancerous and do not spread.

biopsy—Removal of a small amount of tissue for microscopic analysis and diagnosis.

cancer cluster—An unusually high number of cancer cases in a particular area.

carcinogen—A chemical or other substance that can cause cancer.

carcinoma—A cancer that begins in epithelial cells which cover or line internal organs and make up the skin.

cauterization—Using heat, extreme cold, electricity, or chemicals to destroy abnormal tissues.

chemotherapy—The use of drugs to kill cancer cells.

chromosome—Made up of DNA and proteins, chromosomes carry genetic information in the form of genes. Normal human cells have twenty-three pairs of chromosomes. One of each pair comes from the mother, the other from the father.

cytogenetiscist—A scientist who analyzes the structure of chromosomes.

deoxyribonucleic acid (DNA)—A large molecule found in every cell that carries an organism's genetic information.

free radicals—Molecules that react very easily with other chemicals in the body and cause biological damage.

genes—Sections of DNA that tell the cell to make a particular protein.

graft-versus-host disease—A condition in which immune cells from a bone marrow donor attack the recipient's tissues.

leukemia—Cancer that affects the blood-forming cells of the bone marrow.

lymphoma—Cancer of the lymphatic system.

malignant—Cancerous, with cells growing out of control.

metastasis—The spread of cancer cells from one part of the body to another.

monoclonal antibody—A molecule that can detect specific proteins on the surface of cells.

mutation—A change in the DNA sequence.

myeloma—Cancer of the plasma cells, a type of white blood cell.

nucleus—The part of the cell that contains the DNA.

oncogene—A gene capable of changing normal cells into cancerous ones. An oncogene is a mutated version of a proto-oncogene.

oncologist—A doctor who specializes in diagnosing and treating cancer.

oncology—The study of cancer.

phytochemicals—Chemical molecules in plants that may help prevent diseases in humans. Also called antioxidants, flavonoids, and isoflavones.

predisposed—To be more susceptible or more likely to be affected by health problems.

primary tumor—A tumor at the original cancer site.

prognosis—The likely outcome of a disease.

protocol—The specific schedule for a patient's chemotherapy.

proto-oncogene—A normal gene that controls cell growth.

relapse—A reappearance of cancer after a disease-free period.

remission—A decrease or disappearance of the signs or symptoms of cancer.

replication—The process of making an identical copy of the DNA in preparation for cell division.

sarcoma—Cancer of the connective tissue, such as bone or muscle.

secondary tumor—A tumor formed away from the original cancer site due to metastasis.

tumor suppressor gene—A gene that prevents out-of-control cell growth.

For More Information

American Cancer Society (ACS)
National Home Office
250 Williams Street
Atlanta, GA 30303
1-800-ACS-2345

National Cancer Institute (NCI)
NCI Public Inquiries Office
6116 Executive Boulevard, Room 3036A
Bethesda, MD 20892-8322
1-800-4-CANCER (1-800-422-6237)

National Coalition for Cancer Survivorship (NCCS)
1010 Wayne Avenue, Suite 770
Silver Spring, MD 20910
(301) 650-9127

National Comprehensive Cancer Network (NCCN)
500 Old York Road, Suite 250
Jenkintown, PA 19046
(215) 690-0300

National Foundation for Cancer Research (NFCR)
4600 East West Highway, Suite 525
Bethesda, MD 20814
1-800-321-CURE (2873)

CancerCare
275 Seventh Avenue, Floor 22
New York, NY 10001
1-800-813-HOPE (4673)

Further Reading

Bozzone, Donna M. *Causes of Cancer*. New York: Chelsea House Publishers, 2007.

Metcalf, Tom, and Gena Metcalf (eds.). *Cancer*. San Diego: Greenhaven, 2007.

Nelson, Sheila, and Ida Walker. *Youth With Cancer: Facing the Shadows*. Philadelphia: Mason Crest Publishers, 2008.

Sarg, Michael J., and Ann D. Gross. *The Cancer Dictionary*. New York: Checkmark Books, 2007.

Silverstein, Alvin. *Cancer*. Minneapolis, Minn.: Twenty-First Century Books, 2006.

Wyborny, Sheila. *Science on the Edge: Cancer Treatments*. San Diego: Blackbirch Press, 2005.

Internet Addresses

American Cancer Society (ACS)

<http://www.cancer.org/>

CancerCare

<http://www.cancercare.org/>

National Cancer Institute (NCI)

<http://www.cancer.gov/>

To Be Me—A Site for Teens with Cancer

<http://www.2bme.org/>

Index